Comedia Series ● No – 43

COMPUTER MEDIA

LIVING AND WORKING WITH COMPUTERS

by Joel Cayford

Comedia Publishing Group
9 Poland Street, London W1V 3DG   Tel: 01-439 2059

Comedia Publishing Group was set up to investigate and monitor the media in Britain and abroad. The aim of the project is to provide basic information, investigate problem areas, and to share the experiences of those working in the field, while encouraging debate about the future development of the media. The opinions expressed in the books in the series are those of the authors, and do not necessarily reflect the views of Comedia. For a list of other Comedia titles see back pages.

First published in 1987 by Comedia Publishing Group
9 Poland Street, London W1V 3DG.

©Comedia and the author

British Library Cataloguing in Publication Data
    Computer Media: living and working with computers
    1. Communications
    I. Title
    621.38   TK5102.5

ISBN 18517800017

Cover Design by John Ingledew

Distributed in the UK by George Philips Ltd., Arndale Road, Lineside Industrial Estate, Littlehampton, W. Sussex
Distributed in Australia by Second Back Row Press, 50 Govett Street, Katoomba, N.S.W. 2780
Distributed in Canada by D.E.C., 229 College Street, Toronto, Ontario

Typeset by Photosetting, 6 Foundry House, Stars Lane, Yeovil, Somerset Tel: Yeovil 23684

Printed in Great Britain by Unwin Brothers Ltd., The Gresham Press, Old Woking, Surrey

CONTENTS

WHO IS THIS BOOK FOR?

Computer media is about how computers are applied and used, and how the software industry affects people.

This book is aimed at several different reading groups:

- interested laypersons
- industrial and trade union activists affected by computer work
- workers and management regularly using computers
- people wanting to buy and use a computer,

approximately in order of priority.

It treats software, the industry, the workers, the organisations, and the "end users" from several different perspectives:

- Chapter 1 explores the myth of computer infallibility, and investigates some of the more problematic applications of computers, such as Star Wars
- Chapter 2 tells the inside story of how management go about applying computers in a typical admin department. It describes the strategies often used, the people involved, and the effect all this has on the employees at risk of redundancy. It also examines the changing role of the DP department in large organisations today
- Chapter 3 is about the creation of computer software on large computer systems. It describes the roles of all the people concerned when a large piece of software is made to meet a customer's needs. The way computer workers can be used and abused is emphasised
- Chapter 4 touches on several issues of more general concern in Britain's software world – the software economy, the safety or otherwise of VDUs, the Data Protection Act

– Chapter 5 uses the experiences and ideas of organisations which have applied computers in the interests of people rather than profit, and puts forward an agenda for social and industrial action in the software world.

Each chapter is a snap shot which emphasises certain aspects and issues – some of which may also be treated in other chapters. It is not intended that the reader should start from the beginning and read to the end. All chapters are in three parts – a brief introduction, the main text plus news items and a point-by-point summary of the arguments made – so it is possible to skim and read the book at different levels.

Why **Computer media**? Today's media studies courses examine the press, radio and television from many perspectives including decision-making, ownership, impact on the public, as well as "content and form". Computers are also used to store and represent information about many aspects of world and human activity. A broad social appreciation of computers demands that this "computer medium" be explored and investigated using the same approach.

This book is a contribution to that investigation.

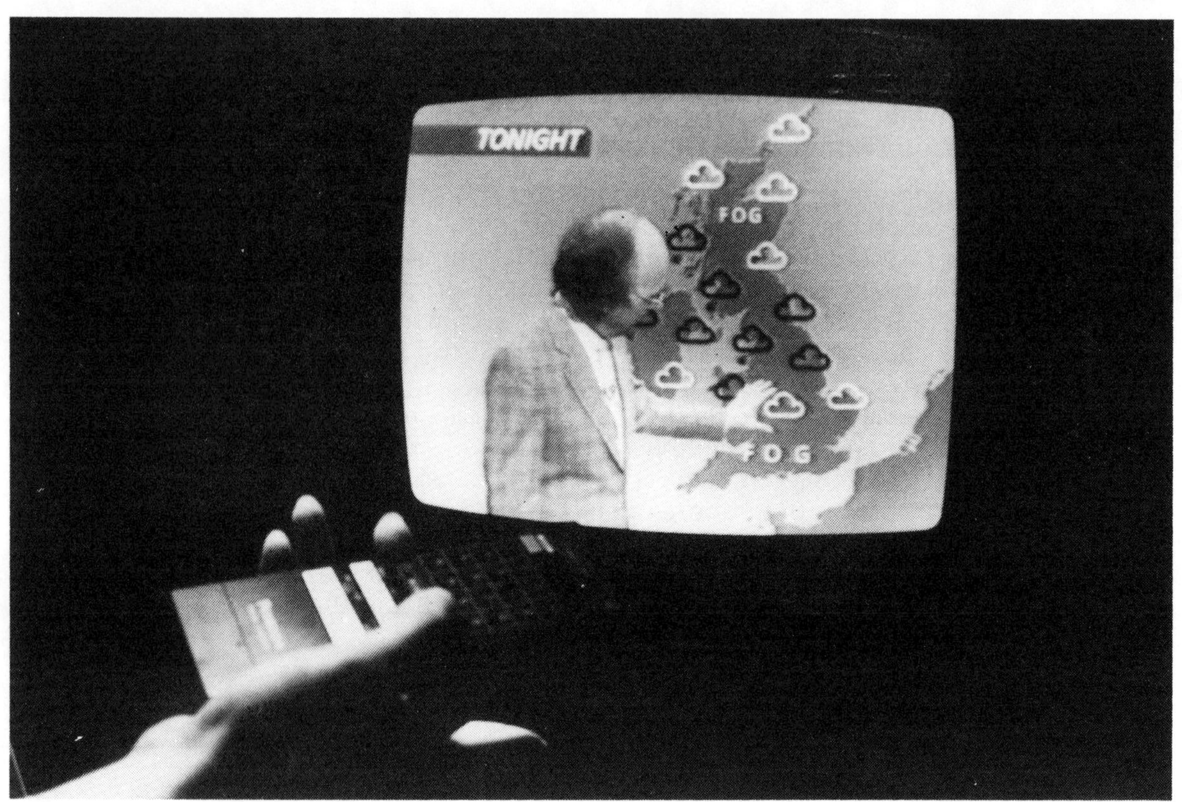

Do you *believe it?*

CONFIDENCE THROUGH COMPUTERS

1

It's when you get a domestic gas bill for £999,943.00 that you begin to understand computers. The next step is the recognition that it's not computers that control people – it's people that control computers. But with today's software sophistication this distinction can become blurred and people PLUS computer get just a little out of control.

Business Modelling is at the small company end of an enormous spectrum of computerised decision-making aids – which today ends at Star Wars. This chapter looks at how assumptions and science are brought together in computer simulations of reality, and asks the question – "Do you believe the weather forecast?"

Computers have clearly been applied in cutting jobs and costs in much of British service and manufacturing industry. Many people have been on the receiving end of such applications. But because computers are such flexible tools – in the hands of flexible people – they are capable of being applied to all sorts of other areas of human activity should the will and the finance be there. One such area is computerised forecasting, prediction and decision-making Some of this work has led to the development of "Expert Systems" and the idea of "Artificial Intelligence".

At their most public we see the results of such labour intensive efforts at simulating reality in television weather forecasts and government predictions from the Treasury Model. On the corporate side there is the shadowy activity of "business modelling" and market forecasting as competing interests strive to gain advantage. In industry and the military, simulations are applied to computer-aided design on the one hand, and to war games on the other. And there are the "troubling" problems of our time ranging from forecasting earthquakes to predicting the safety of underground nuclear waste disposal – all of which rely on computer software projects financed by government departments seeking answers.

These sorts of problems have several things in common – they are extremely complicated with hundreds of interrelating variables to consider, and because they all look into the crystal ball they have to take account of chance. Difficult enough for a poker player worrying about a ten-pound bet – but staking society on the outcome of a dumb computer! Approaching the analysis and understanding of problems like these demands the answers to questions like:

- what do we know now?
- what can we assume?
- what if ...?

Answers to the first two may lead to hundreds of pieces of "information", "fact", or "feeling" being listed. The last question is actually tens, hundreds or even thousands of questions – What if this happens? What if that happens? What if we're wrong? In the days before computers many of the applications listed above were very much under study and consideration by teams of "qualified" people in offices with piles of paper, furiously turning out report after report. But the difficulty inherent in the sheer volume of information compounded by the vast number of possible outcomes meant that the decision-making process was continually frustrated by doubt because "we haven't considered all the possibilities". In practice, decisions *were* made but were often described as having "low confidence".

Computers have provided today's researchers with an information sorting, testing, manipulating and retrieval power beyond their wildest dreams – apparently overcoming many of their problems in aiding and abetting the decision-makers. But just how "expert" are these software systems? How are they made? Who uses them? What are their shortcomings? And how are they used to manipulate public opinion?

WEATHER FORECASTING

Everybody seems to want to know reliably what the weather will do tomorrow, next week, this summer, next winter, and so on. Even today very fundamental decisions such as how much seed grain should be planted out or kept in store are based on weather predictions. From the private – shall we have a picnic? – to the public – will the demo be a success? – to the military – is it better to drop the bomb on a sunny day or a rainy day? – people and organisations rely on their weather expert's forecasts.

In fact the "science" of meteorology is one of the most complex of all – especially when attempting to forecast tomorrow's weather throughout Britain, for example. The amount of information involved is vast and the possible interactions and their effects are infinitely variable. From observation, meteorologists know what combination of air pressure, air temperature and water presence is likely to produce snow, for example – but that is very different from predicting when that combination will occur and exactly where it will occur in any part of the atmosphere above Britain.

Typically science learns from its mistakes and each time an incorrect weather prediction is made the forecasters re-examine the assumptions used to arrive at the forecast, and seek to modify those rules so the same mistake won't be repeated. This process has been going on for centuries. A huge archive of this sort of weather information is kept. It is continuously being raked over in the search for "patterns" and "clues", as new arrivals to the field of meteorology test out their ideas on "what leads to this or that weather condition". Each weather forecast relies heavily on these assumptions and also on the steady stream of "current" information being provided by satellites, met. stations, ship reports and airline pilot reports. The storage, co-ordination, analysis and presentation of **all** these data has been an impossible task until only very recently with the production of very large computers.

Today we are treated to all the benefits this technology offers when we watch the computer-generated weather maps on television. But how often is it right? Would you stake a crucial decision on computer-generated rain clouds? Do you feel you could more or less predict tomorrow's weather yourself as reliably as the massed ranks of met. stations and computerised forecasts that end up on television?

Most of us have a healthy disrepect for weather forecasts because we are constantly in touch with the reality of the weather. Our experience tells us that weather forecasts are often wrong. Yet today many political and business decisions are based on the predictions of other computer models which work in much the same way as weather forecasting software.

BUSINESS MODELLING

A Business Model is a computer program which more or less accurately simulates the operation of a business over a period of time. At its simplest a model might represent a manufacturing business as a series of flows of materials and money in response to a predicted demand for its products over the next year. Thus the model begins with the sales prediction of the anticipated annual demand. This might be expressed as the projected orders in each of fifty-two weeks – with orders down in summer and up in autumn, for example. The model would show this demand being met by lowering the stocks of the product made by the business. In parallel with this the model would hold stocks of raw materials which would be depleted as the production line converted them into products to top up finished product stocks. Money flows would be modelled using a "water reservoir" to simulate the bank balance – with increasing orders causing the level to rise (after a suitable payment delay), and increasing production causing the level to fall as wages and overtime are paid and new raw materials are purchased.

Such a model allows management to explore the effects of delays in payment, the phasing of production (doing it in batches, day work, or twenty-four-hour shift work), the benefits of delaying delivery to customers, the savings in keeping raw material stock levels down set against the possibility of running out in times of high production.

A Business Model is a computer program which allows the complex interrelationships of an organisation to be explored according to the information and assumptions provided, and according to the skills of system analyst and programmer staff in actually putting these things into the computer. It is an application of computers where the phrase "garbage in – garbage out" has a lot of truth. Models can go into a great deal of detail – looking at every single operation in the production process or every step in an over-the-counter transaction – or in a very generalised way as described above. Financial modelling is very important to organisations involved in buying and selling – especially when operating internationally. In such models the "demand" assumptions will seek to take account of possible "political changes" or "economic developments" which would affect the performance of a business operation.

It is in such areas of uncertainty that a Business Model is often used as a decision aid because of its ability to handle quickly "what-if" questions. Let's assume a business model has pro-grammed into it the company strategy and plans for the year ahead. It would therefore encapsulate the best thinking of company decision-makers and serve as a focus for them to consult, discuss and agree company plans. One of the key projections they will examine is predicted profit or loss. But before they do that they need to assure themselves that the model is "robust". There are two aspects to this and the first is that the model should as accurately as required reflect the organisation's structure and plans, and the second is that the model should operate "realistically" in a variety of possible commercial situations. To test the latter quality the company operations people will come up with an "optimistic market prediction", a "pessimistic market prediction", and other predictions of sales for the year ahead. What they will want to see is that the business model will cope with their varying fears over what the year might hold in store, without sending the company bankrupt or into any other undesirable chasm. It should be noted that the model might treat staff levels in much the same way as money levels – thus they would rise and fall with order levels, for example!

News Story
Report on computerised intelligence gathering:
"Good predictions on political stability are vital to potential business ventures, especially in Third World countries where both the profits and risks to be taken can be immense. To ensure wise business decisions, therefore, multinationals are now susbscribing more to private concerns which can offer 'political risk analysis'.

"US-based International reporting Information Systems (IRIS) is the largest of these. One of their London-based reps spoke of the Falklands situation, 'Some very clever people seemed to think that invasion by the Argentinians was liable to take place and that there might be a freeze on Argentinian funds in the UK. That meant that anyone doing business with Argentina moved such funds before the crisis began. This is just the sort of information IRIS can provide.'"

(Computing, *8/7/82)*

If the model works "realistically" while reacting to their various future scenarios they will gain confidence in their plans – provided they have confidence in the model itself. Thus a Business Model serves a range of purposes:

- it serves to represent how the company works as agreed by the managers collectively in consultation with programmer staff
- it allows for detailed experimentation with company operations without fiddling with the actual company
- it enables ideas and plans to be tested to check their effects on company operations and financial performance
- it provides pointers to those parts of the company plan which are most sensitive, and therefore require most attention.

At its most beneficial a Business Model serves as a focus for the views and ideas of all involved in making decisions and preparing plans for the company future. Because it requires that people meet and articulate their feelings in enough detail to be inserted into the model, then a major side-effect is that everybody gets to hear what everybody else is thinking – rather like computer-aided consultation where the discussions are the editorial process in creating a computer representation of the company. Once a model is running the "results and predictions" it produces usually serve to raise questions about the model (and hence about the company), so it is refined in parallel with the collective growth of people's understanding of what the organisation is doing.

Problems with Business Models begin when the "powers that be" take control, minimise the consultative process, and rely on the model itself as a decision-making tool. The reasoning behind this move is that the business model has encapsulated all of the expertise and business acumen of its collective editorial team, and can therefore be deemed to act on their behalf. It is at this point that the computer takes control and people take a back seat. The results and predictions of a computerised business model only make sense in the context of the assumptions the model is based on. The perfect graphics and number filled tables that constitute the computer forecasts can look impressive and create comfort – yet they are meaningless without a full understanding of the perfectly human assumptions and feelings that collectively produced them.

ECONOMIC MODELS

It is hard to know for sure what the effect of a number, a percentage, a table, or a graph is on people reading the paper or watching television. These days we are blitzed with statistics, forecasts, indicators and economic model predictions – most of them produced and presented for our consumption by a computer. And most of them aimed at backing up someone's point of view.

The government's "Treasury Model" of the British economy spits out quite a lot of the numbers used by governments in justifying their courses of action. How accurate or meaningful are these numbers? In fact an Economy Model is very similar to a Business Model in structure and preparation. The main differences lie in the huge number of additional variables required to describe "an economy" and the variety of economic theories and philosophies that can be applied.

Any government has a set of objectives – some unstated. These will point to the adoption of a certain approach to the economy – and hence the preferred theory. This theory will form the structural backbone of the Economy Model and constitute its assumptions. From that point on the model will be tweaked and fiddled to produce the best outcome in line with the objectives. As time passes and experience is gained in applying the economic theory, the model will be altered – possibly structurally – in line with government policy and objective changes. Any published results and predictions will be carefully selected and edited – some will be used to show how accurate the model is by listing past predictions, while others will point to the future. This is a careful balancing act designed to increase public confidence in the model so that future predictions (and hence the government) will be taken seriously.

Economic changes and developments involve millions of people, thousands of social groups, hundreds of countries, and vast numbers of material considerations. Predicting the future of a country's economy is at least as complex as predicting the weather. Do people feel the same about government statistics and predictions as they do about television weather forecasts? Would that change if some effort was made to share the assumptions lying behind the model with the public?

WAR GAMES

Computers were invented to deal with some of the technical problems that confront people who build machines to fight wars. It is no coincidence that the most imaginative and creative (!) uses of computers today are by the military. This short examination of the software side of military computing looks at two important aspects:

- "onboard" computing used in self-targeting weapons (e.g., Cruise)
- computing used in command and control systems (e.g., army battlefield control and Star Wars).

Much of today's military hardware is computer guided – anti-submarine torpedoes, anti-aircraft missiles, anti-missile missiles, Cruise missiles, and ship gun systems depend totally on "dedicated" computers to search out and destroy their targets. Creating the software that goes into these computers – many of which are about the size of a hand calculator – is an incredibly demanding and skilled job. Much of the software design work is done using a separate computer program which fully simulates the envisaged weapon in operation. Thus a computer model of the design-weapon is programmed into a typical office-housed computer. Part of this model is a simulation of the logic of the weapon's own computerised command and control computer. In a previous section a Business Model was described as being driven by the predicted demand for its products – and the model examined how the business would respond to that demand. Similarly a simulation of a weapon system also examines the response to a demand – the demands made by a simulated enemy target. The weapon must be able to respond "effectively" to all the demands the target can make. And it is in this area that the greatest amount of "creativity" lies. The weapon system designers have to list every anticipated action that the enemy target might or could take to evade the weapon. These actions, along with the proposed performance of the weapon, constitute the assumptions that lie behind the weapon control system computer program logic. This is why the "enemy" are always keen to capture unexploded samples so that they can strip out the computer program, decode it and discover the state of their opponent's thinking. Then they can respond by training their own personnel (or reprogramming their systems) to evade the weapon using a tactic not already anticipated.

Tactics and strategies are crucial in guided weapons, and they are critical in battle control involving thousands of people, hundreds of weapons and distances of thousands of miles – where a delay of one second by one person can now mean the difference between "winning" and "losing". Whereas guided weapons are fairly easy to test (in the backyard or by selling them to countries fighting a war), there has not been an opportunity to pit East against West in a substantial conflict of a non-nuclear nature. To replace this, each side fights the other endlessly in a series of computerised war games, and just as with guided weapons the

War Games and Arcade Games learn from each other

most important thing to get right is anticipating all the variations of how the other side will react. These war games are fiddled and tweaked just like the Treasury Model of the economy – and provide results just as dependent on the assumptions driving the model. Today the Western military spend hundreds of millions of pounds on computer software and ergonomic development (ergonomy is the study of the relationship between people and the machines they use to get the "best" result). Because conventional wars still involve people the military are preoccupied with ensuring that their workers alongside their computerised command and control systems form a united organic body. A sign of these developments is the similarity between arcade games and military control systems – where user friendliness has been taken to an extreme.

Computer software is absolutely critical to military activities today. It is used in virtually all its machines and all its command systems. And it plays a crucial role for system design and development in the form of simulation and modelling tools.

And so we come to Star Wars. No one really knows what Stars Wars is yet, but the project seems to consist of a combination of offensive space-launched missile systems and defensive anti-missile laser systems. Since nobody – or hardly anybody – is envisaged as orbiting with these systems it is planned that the whole thing will be controlled by computer – "failsafe" of course.

The main technical objections to the feasibility of such a system are as follows:

- the possible variations in "enemy tactics" are so great that the software required would be the biggest computer program ever made, and would inevitably contain errors
- it will not be possible to produce "error free" software without testing it in "real world" situations.

To be "useful" the Star War system would have to be able to respond to an "enemy missile launch" within a few seconds without human interaction. It would be permanently switched on. Do we have reason to trust it? How many Cruise missiles have flown into hills and trees? How many seagulls have been blasted by anti-aircraft missiles? How many whales have been mistaken for submarines? Such accidents are commonplace during system design and testing. How could Star Wars be tested? The fact that there is a risk of similar accidents, even when these weapons are brought into service is almost accepted as normal. But what if Star Wars "thought" Chernobyl was a missile launch?

> *News Story*
> *Parliamentary report on Star Wars:*
> *"Linlithgow Labour MP Tam Dalyell denounced Star Wars as 'a game of celestial snooker'. He claimed that scientists at Edinburgh University's department of Artificial Intelligence made it clear to MoD officials their objections to doing SDI work. They felt it would divert the research community from more relevant social and industrial work. He warned,'the difficulty, they say, is that in the absence of a spare planet which the MoD does not have there is no way of testing SDI'."*
>
> *(Computing, 1986)*

QUALITY ASSURANCE

For many organisations and people it is critically important that they feel able to "trust" what their computer programs do. Most banks rely totally on computer systems to handle millions of electronic transactions for their customers and to get the sums right. The hardware must work and the software has to be "error free". Quality Assurance is the term used to describe the management methods used to organise the software production so that errors and mistakes are minimised (or eliminated). For some systems – such as accounting systems – it is possible to test the software very thoroughly and to build it according to certain guidelines so there is very little likelihood of there being a hidden error. Even so the most popular accounting software systems available on desktop micros today are still revealing the odd error after being on the market for years and after selling thousands of copies.

In the 1960s and early 1970s it was generally felt by managers that the "quality" of software was largely determined by the "quality" of the programmers who made it. Today, where software takes years to make, those attitudes have given way to organised and managed approaches to software development. Quality Control and Quality Assurance are part of these approaches. The following definition of quality assurance is loosely based on one provided in a Ministry of Defence document intended for suppliers entitled *Guide to the Achievement of Quality in Software*:

> "Software Quality assurance is a planned and systematic set of actions to provide confirmation that software products meet the end user's stated requirements, and will continue to do so as long as the requirements remain unchanged. It includes the full development process including definition of the product (specifications), definition of the development process (codes of practice) and control of the development process (quality control)."

Taking up the example of accounting software again, if there were mistakes in the "completed" software then the fault in the QA process is likely to be during the "control of the development process" since the specifications will have been drawn from standard and well understood accounting practice. Where the use of full QA is becoming increasingly important is in the development of "critical software". Every software maker feels their software is critical to them, but some software is critical socially – for example Star Wars software and the software used to assess the safety of underground nuclear waste disposal. The governments of Britain, Canada and the United States have all awarded lucrative contracts to their nuclear industry for the writing of software to simulate the underground burial of nuclear waste. They want a prediction that shows it's safe – but they also want a simulation that will be believed. Their simulations are just like complicated business models – the differences being:

- the simulations have to look 25,000 years into the future
- the assumptions are based on almost no experience
- the consequences for society of getting it wrong.

The main risk with underground waste disposal is water soaking into the containers, dissolving out whatever is in them, and then flowing into nearby lakes and streams. To simulate this risk the "risk assessment program engineering" process has to include the expertise of geologists, geophysicists, hydrologists, structural engineers, chemical engineers – not to mention computer programmers – and bring the whole lot together in a credible way. In this sort of application the development process is not the main problem. The main problem is in specifying what happens to contained waste underground so that a program can be designed in the first place. In fact the QA process in Canada (where they have decided against underground waste disposal) involved a national committee of engineers, politicians, academics and concerned members of the public who were all free to scrutinise all aspects of the simulation. Criticism and comment led to changes in the simulation and to changes in the level of confidence held in the simulation itself and in the concept of nuclear waste disposal underground.

So while the method of QA was aimed at the development of the software programs – the real measure of "quality" was how confident people felt about their own sub-models and what the simulation was telling them generally. The committee consultation process served to break down the departmental barriers of professionalism and expertise so all involved could get a feel for all of the issues and technical considerations. In this way the Canadian waste disposal simulation functioned rather like a Business Model in focusing attention on all of the problems. In this software-centred investigation QA was regarded as crucial by the commissioning government departments because they were aware that in citing the results of a computer model as evidence in support of a decision to go ahead with underground waste disposal, they would need to be very sure that the software was correct in every detail.

One idea for increasing confidence in such studies is to commission two entirely separate simulation projects – each with their own team of "experts" – and compare their predictions. The reasons why this approach is not commonly adopted are; cost, the problems of reconciling the inevitable differences, the scarcity of experts, and the fact that differences will usually boil down to differences of opinion between the experts anyway. Better to choose sympathetic experts and let them speak through a single soothsayer simulation!

EXPERT SYSTEMS AND ARTIFICIAL INTELLIGENCE

The idea behind an "Expert System" is to get a computer program to act as a substitute for an expert. The argument goes as follows – if the reasoning behind an expert's thinking is logical then the decision-making process can be represented as a complete system and therefore made into a computer program. There are at least a couple of types of Expert System:

- computer software which embodies expertise
- computer software which absorbs expertise.

There are many examples of the former category – accounting software embodies the expertise of a double-entry bookkeeper, cash vending machine software uses the same rules that bank tellers use in dispensing cash, and certain medical diagnostic software packages enable GPs to perform as specialist consultants. To create this sort of software it is necessary to extract the embodied expertise from real live experts (or books), and represent it in computer software so it can be used by the people it is intended for. Thus an asthma diagnosis package might start by asking the doctor to enter the background information about the patient – sex and age, for example – then physiological information – temperature, blood pressure, breathing rate, weight – then more specific questions – pains, allergies, etc. In this way the Expert System would guide the doctor's investigation while making constant reference to its own computer data about the whys and wherefores of asthma. The system might be programmed to provide suggestions to the doctor for further tests, to present a possible diagnosis, or to make recommendations for treatment. Its operation will be entirely dependent on the views of the people who programmed it, and also on the assumption that it is possible to represent all the types of asthma sufferers in one single system.

The latter category of Expert System starts as a system empty of expertise. It is a computer program designed to act as an expert in any field which can be defined by a rigid and complete set of computerised rules. Here the idea is you don't have to be an expert in programming yourself – yet the system enables you to represent your own expertise in an Expert System. In practice these empty Expert Systems tend to reflect the analytical processes of the people who made them, and cannot be made to understand rules governing areas of expertise which fall outside these programmers' experiences. Among the questions Expert System makers have to answer are:

- –can expertise be boiled down to rules?
- –what are the basic types of rules?
- –how do rules interact?

Early investigations into Expert Systems ran into various stumbling blocks:

- –how to handle situations where the rules are not all known?
- –how to cope with new information once the Expert System is made?
- –how to get the Expert System to "learn" from mistakes?

It wasn't long before such questions encouraged researchers into referring to their work as "Artificial Intelligence". Hardly surprising when you consider that the questions they were asking of their computer programs are the same questions put to scientists working to understand how the human mind works. And this is where the efforts at Artificial Intelligence break down. Because we don't know how our own mental processes work, then it sets the programmers trying to copy the mind – an impossible task.

Today the opponents and proponents of "AI" (as Artificial Intelligence is known) are locked in debates about its possibility/impossibility. Some of these debates have led to imaginative definitions of AI – Alan Turing, a famous mathematician and logician (died in 1954) proposed his test of artificial intelligence: "if a user, typing and seeing information at a computer cannot tell whether he is conversing with a computer or with another human being, the computer can be called intelligent". Turing's definition is not helpful in telling us what he thought "conversing with a human being" involves . . .

22

Summary

- *computers reflect the assumptions, ideas and opinions of the people who make the software programs*
- *computers are very useful in sifting through mountains of information using software "filters" made by researchers*
- *the computer software and approaches used in weather forecasting, Business Modelling and the government Treasury Model are very similar, with similarly reliable results*
- *the Military depend heavily on computer simulations to "test" new designs and actual systems in the absence of war*

- *Star Wars technology is crucially dependent on a computer program so big and complex it would be impossible to get one hundred per cent accuracy*
- *investigations into nuclear waste disposal rely heavily on the results of computer simulations whose accuracy is controlled through "Quality Assurance"*
- *Expert Systems are useful for simple applications like car engine fault diagnosis, and helpful as guides in medical diagnosis*
- *Artificial Human Intelligence is a myth.*

Computer room in the Inland Revenue

ICL Press Photo

COST CUTTING COMPUTERISATION 2

We see banks of flickering equipment cabinets and the odd tape spool rotating backwards and forwards. The lights are fluorescent and there is the quiet hum of cooling fans. You catch a glimpse of a human being pressing a key. The typical image of an organisation's computer department conceals far more than it reveals. Why is it there? What does it do? Where is everybody? What are they doing?

Corporate computerisation is about change. It's a long hard slog which affects everybody in the organisation from top to bottom, and rarely results in the ice-cool efficiency of the media stereotype. This chapter explores the motivations, actions and reactions of all concerned as a company takes the "paper-less" office leap.

All organisations large and small have to deal with a number of very ordinary details for every one of their employees:

- –personal details
- –pay
- –tax
- –NHS payments
- –pension details,

and there are usually others:

- –holiday details
- –training requirements
- –promotion prospects
- –family details
- –expenses and perks.

Even if an organisation only employs twenty people with a changeover rate of say four staff per year – administering the above manually is very time consuming, often boring and very important to get one hundred per cent accurate. Not very long ago over a million people did this work in Britain's companies – let alone the public sector. It was the easiest activity to computerise because it was so well understood, so clear and compartmentalised – the workers had made it so. Their job satisfaction was pride in their organisation and their accuracy, and pride in the speed with which their system could produce the information required by management. But their work has always been seen very much as an overhead, not contributing to profits only creating a cost, and therefore the target for cuts wherever possible.

Over the last fifteen years there has been a rush to computerise company administration systems. Apart from sheer cost-cutting opportunity there was the additional race to stay ahead of competitors and even gain commercial advantage over them.

So, let's follow the steps taken by a typical organisation of a few hundred employees as it goes about computerising its admin department. This explanation is based on what happens now. But it is instructive to put these events into the context of the last couple of decades of computer industry development, and hence there are digressions into recent history.

THE FINANCIAL ARGUMENTS

In the early days companies moved into computers partly because of the savings, and partly because of the "high tech" image that went with it. Fast talking company directors loved to be able to refer in passing to their new toy – and very glamorous it was to be seen using the new technology. But computers were relatively expensive a decade ago – so buying had to be justified by more substantial arguments than just improving the company image. Over the years a range of "winning arguments" have been tried and proven for "overcoming customer objections" to buying into computer technology. Today's slick consultants rely heavily on the "cost justification" argument.

The projected costs of computerisation are presented under several headings to describe the initial outlay:

- –outright purchase cost of hardware
- –outright purchase cost of software
- –outfitting of computer room

     –installation and testing of computer
     –setting up client software system
     –training client staff
     –handover,

and a further set of headings for subsequent annual running costs:

     –hardware maintenance agreement
     –software support agreement
     –insurance (hardware, software and data)
     –computer magnetic storage media and paper
     –computer system operator wages.

The consultants will also conduct a full investigation of the company's present manual system – the aim being to work out exactly how much it is costing them to run their administration pre-computerisation. In this analysis much is made about "the cost to the company of mistakes and the worry of legal action" – the implication being that computers don't make mistakes.
  So, the "current costs" will be presented:

     –labour costs
     –annual recruitment costs
     –floor space and other overhead costs
     –additional staff costs (NH admin, training)
     –estimated cost to company of mistakes.

The consultant will then calculate how many years it will take for the recommended computer substitute to "pay for itself", and for the "first real savings to be made". In fact, many companies simply cannot afford to buy or run their own computer. Recognising this market encouraged a number of existing computer owners to offer computer time by the second to computer-less companies which could gain access to it by visiting from time to time, or by communicating with a VDU over a phone line.
  In the early days of computing IBM used to rent its costly computers to customers on a three-month return basis. After a while IBM got into difficulties because customers did return them since new ones were on the market, and IBM couldn't do anything with a growing pile of second-hand ones. So it switched to outright sales. Specialist office equipment companies then bought stocks of new IBM computers and leased them to potential IBM customers. This system suited customers very well – the lease payments were tax deductible, and they could sell the leased machine back to the lease company to take up another lease on a bigger (or smaller) machine when they wanted to. Initially it suited IBM since they were selling machines – albeit to lease companies – but later it saw its customers turning in droves to lease companies,

to cheap computing and to second-hand computers. So IBM went into the lease market too, initially offering better terms than the lease companies in an attempt to squeeze them out of business. IBM can do this because it has the financial clout to stand losses and manipulate the market, to starve competitors or "parasites", and finally to force customers to pay top prices for "newer and better" computers.

SELLING COMPUTERISATION

Apart from being expensive, computerising company administration is also very complex and time-consuming. Many of those who suffered and learnt from managing such projects recognised the value of their experience to others and set up special computer software companies – some of which today employ hundreds of programmers, analysts and consultants.

Earlier in this section one of these consultants is described preparing the ground for computerisation. This outsider would be looking to handle the computer and software purchase through their own company and to collect a percentage rakeoff. Such a company would also employ a team of workers specialising in "conversion jobs" ready to provide the expertise and labour needed during computerisation.

Not so long ago these companies did not exist. The people who did the selling were the computer manufacturers' salespeople. Their interests were in selling as many computers as possible – the commissions were very high – they were not concerned about administration software or any other form of software since early computer manufacturers did not tend to make applications software. And they usually had very little knowledge of how a typical company actually worked either.

These salespeople very quickly learned there was no point in talking to the managers of admin departments. Firstly because the computer seller could never be bothered to understand what the admin department actually did, and second because the manager usually saw the spectre of computerisation as a threat to their jobs (let alone their employees' jobs). The most effective salespeople directed their sales pitches at board level where cost-justifications, quality, high tech imagery, and general computer wizardry could be placed in front of uneducated directors fearful of being left behind. The existence of good, ready-made software usually made the sale easier to complete, but even without it the salespeople often pressed home the sale by encouraging the board to "recruit a Data Processing manager, get in a few programmers and build yourselves a system".

Additional "investment arguments" will also be put:

- invest in computers, the technology is here to stay
- invest in IBM, or ICL, etc., and keep ahead of the rest (see later)
- the sooner you start the sooner you'll benefit from the savings.

Across the country computers were purchased, software was purchased, and programmers were recruited. As much as £1,000,000 would have been spent even in average sized companies. But there were very few quick and easy success stories.

THE MISTAKES THEY MADE

The typical mistakes made during computerisation – many of which are still being repeated today – include:

- underestimating the sophistication and complexity of the old manual system, and hence underestimating the computerisation problem
- underestimating the problem of producing good software, and ending up by producing an unreliable white elephant for an admin system
- underestimating the amount of skilled labour needed to create an effective software system and to run it subsequently
- overestimating the ability of purchased software to handle the activities and operations embodied in the old manual system
- assuming that EVERY aspect of the old system will be computerised, and that ALL paperwork will cease
- failing to recognise the new problems computerising presents
- keeping old records, repairing mistakes discovered "too late", and the "arms length" nature of magnetic data storage ("Why can't I get at it?")
- wrongly estimating the size of the administration department's work – or its rate of change – and hence buying a computer system which is too big or too small.

The industry and its journals – *Computing*, *Computer Weekly*, *Computer Talk* and *Datalink* – buzz with DP department tales of shock and horror as yet more unsuspecting admin departments and computer workers take the plunge. But who gets affected – and what are these effects?

WHAT ABOUT THE PEOPLE?

In spite of the popular view that "working in admin is boring", for many people who work in a company's personnel and records department there is often satisfaction in their office job, along with the comfortable presence of fellow workers with whom the daily batch of problems can be discussed and dealt with. Over the fifty or so years it may have taken the company to grow to its present size – possibly employing fifty in its admin department – there will have been hundreds upon hundreds of subtle changes in the working practices to handle changing and expanding demands. The nature of many of these changes and the very reasons for them will often have been lost, and unconcerned by this the department continues to do its job as an essential and developing organ within the company body.

It's not just the fear of an unknown technology and job loss that upsets this department when computerisation approaches – it's more often the activities of the "razor-edged" computer analyst or consultant probing into the deepest and darkest entrails of the department which is felt as the greatest threat. The endless questions and the closest examination of shut-forever filing cabinet drawers, the discovery of personal systems and the exhuming of long forgotten "repairs" – all create an atmosphere of dismay and anxiety. And this is long before a computer terminal is even sighted. Anger is also generated, particularly when the investigation is cursory and fails to gain a full understanding of why things are done in certain ways, and what is really involved in different people's jobs. A human resourced admin department will inevitably develop a human centred approach. Individuals will be trusted to take decisions affecting employees' lives. Their experience is appreciated and their judgement respected – but the precise details of what they do will often not be appreciated – let alone be readily programmed into a computer!

Sometimes top management will be quite doubtful if a computer is needed at all. To be sure though, they will want to analyse their admin department, but in a way that will avoid raising anyone's fears. Here the analysis will have to masquerade under the cover of some other activity:

      –rewriting everybody's job description
      –reorganising the department (e.g., by separating out typing)
      –shifting admin to other rooms in the company,

Old technology with a human touch

most of which provide the opportunity of "getting someone in to sleuth the admin department". Why not just ask the admin manager – you ask? Often they don't know much about the detail of the work done – their role has become more one of "man management" and "getting in another temp".

Management knows it is crucial for any manual system to function smoothly – especially while it is being computerised. If a key objective is to lay off manual system staff then management will be anxious not to raise the alarm until the new computer system is trusted. It is usually during the changeover period that a company is most vulnerable to strike action by manual system staff. In most cases it's the only weapon an admin department has to defend itself with, but generally no organised defence is mounted as the reliable nine to fivers – continuing to believe "management wouldn't do that to us after what we've done for them" – co-operate and reveal the secrets of their work.

Meanwhile the admin department managers and supervisors in the middle are not sure who their allies are:

> –is it the workers, "they are as anxious as I am"?
> –is it the computer people, "to be safe, I should be one of them"?
> –is it senior management, "they need someone who knows the ropes"?

At the end of it all a specification will emerge from the consultancy company forming the basis of the computerisation recommendation. The next step for the company is to decide what computer and software combination to buy.

WHICH COMPUTER?

This is a nightmare decision for any company – especially in the days before computers could be leased. At least £500,000 might have to be spent on a lump of hardware. Who to ask? Whose advice to believe? A pragmatic first step was often:

> "We know we want a computer. There's only a few to choose from. So, let's get their salespeople in and see what they have to say. See what deals they have to offer."

And the computer majors would be contacted and presentations arranged – "Our place or yours?" – "Would you like lunch?" – Can we send someone to talk this over with you first?" – are some of the subtle beginnings from the salespeople, each trying to gain an upper hand and to understand the potential customer's deepest concerns.

One of the key sales strategies for the salespeople when they are in a competitive situation for the custom of a company goes like this: "Find out the extent of the contact's computer knowledge. Because it's important not to create problems that are not there (in the customer's mind) already. But be aware of the importance of being the first to reveal new information. The customer respects the supplier that tells the truth – the whole truth – but at the right time."

Underlying this strategy is the salespeople's idea – "a little knowledge is a dangerous thing". In fact computers are very complex machines and trying to filter from all of the myriads of operational and performance characteristics those relevant to your intended application is a difficult task even for people with considerable computer expertise. On top of that, what is an advantage in a computer in one application may be a disadvantage or not required in another.

For the managers such presentations often serve to provide them with the general criteria that can be applied in deciding what to buy and where to get it. Thus informed they can direct a strong line of questioning at the hungry computer salespeople:

- how much is it?
-what extras are needed and what do they cost?
-what software is available for it?
-how easy is it to operate?
-where are the people who know how to work it?
-who should we use to get our system into it?
-how can it be expanded to handle our growth?
-how new is its technology?
-when will it be superseded?
-will your new products run the old software?
-who is using them now?
-do you mind if we contact them for a chat?
-what after sales service do you offer?
-what software services do you offer?
-how much service are we likely to need?

In parallel with this the company may seek a range of "professional" opinions, and they may recruit someone with appropriate experience to help with both the purchase decision and the implementation.

COMPUTER SALES AND MARKETING STRATEGIES

Up to now the story has unfolded as if it's the computer-buying company which calls the tune when dealing with the computer manufacturers. In most cases of computer purchase nothing could be further from the truth. Since the computer hardware industry is very profitable and since many of the competing products are broadly similar, then it's down to the most effective marketing and selling methods to ensure customers buy from particular manufacturers. This has led to various aggressive marketing tactics which are more about coercing companies to buy into computing, rather than gently waiting for telephone calls arranging sales presentations.

IBM has been the league leader of such activities for most of its thirty-odd years making and selling computers, and here we

IBM Press Photo

digress briefly to consider some of its most notable methods of persuading the customer into the IBM fold.

NUMBER ONE. The blue suited and beardless salesman calls on a company and offers to carry out a free survey of the company's business potential. Flattered by the attention of a successful multinational and being assured that the advice is free, the company agrees. The completed survey is positive about the business and makes a point of recommending they **don't** buy a new computer because their current systems are effective enough. The IBM rep then departs leaving behind a company which will treat other computer salespeople with curt dismissals – "Who needs you when IBM tells us we don't need a computer?" Several months go by, and the IBMer drops in again. "Yes, we'd love another survey!" This time, due to improved management and a business upturn, the survey recommends investment in a new computer system. The sale is easy with only a whiff of uninformed competition. The success of this approach is that it identifies potential customers, gets a foot in the door, and keeps the competition away.

NUMBER TWO. Computer technology always appears to be changing, expanding, making new leaps. This generates concern over when to buy – how long to wait. In 1968 rumours of a new IBM computer began to fly. Companies wanting computers hung back. The rumours continued and IBM's competitors became angry –

News Story
Report on IBM Strategy for Dealing with Compatible PC Competitors:

"There are several thrusts:
- *regularly change the technology to keep the costs of keeping pace high*
- *bind PC dealers into IBM with special exclusive deals to control distribution*
- *protect patents and copyright with 'vigorous' legal action*
- *aggressively orchestrate price cuts and price hikes to squeeze competitors*
- *defend large corporate customers by warning of 'computer communications problems in future'*
- *create unease in the market-place by warning of new developments and new prices..."*

(Computing, *15/5/86)*

their sales slumped. Eventually Control Data (US computer manufacturer) launched an action against IBM under US anti-trust law. It took five years to settle. At the same time the US government also took anti-trust action against IBM. That case lasted fourteen years before being dropped! Recently the EEC has had a variety of European legal battles with IBM. And what happens? Win or lose IBM is seen to be arrogantly sure of itself and its products – and keeps its new developments to itself while the embers of rumour are fanned. Other computer manufacturers label the effect of such behaviour on the market as the FUD factor – Fear, Uncertainty and Doubt. The more of it there is, the more likely that people will buy IBM because it feels solid, dependable and strong in a FUD-filled climate.

NUMBER THREE. As a general rule computer manufacturers want to go on selling computers. In the last decade their main challenge has been getting customers to upgrade, to expand, to buy more add-ons – generally to get rid of the old one and buy a new one. Once a company has decided to change there is a free-for-all as rival computer manufacturers line up for the business. And it's at this point the enormous problem of converting a crucially important computerised system from one computer to another has to be faced. Rivals wanting the company to change manufacturer will play the difficulty down, while the current system manufacturer will play it up – "stick with us, our systems are upwards compatible, don't give yourself a headache". In fact all manufacturers play this game, at the heart of which is the computer operating system and whatever application software is being used.

WHAT ABOUT THE OPERATING SYSTEM?

For a detailed explanation of what an Operating System does, the reader is referred to Appendix 2. Briefly, an Operating System consists of a set of special software programs which run the computer itself – the memory, the VDUs, the processor, and any other pieces of attached equipment. This software is effectively the computer's lifeblood, while the applications software (databases, payroll, word-processing, etc.) are its brains. Each major computer manufacturer has developed its own computer operating system – not only that but each model of their computer uses subtle variants on the "base" operating system – often incompatible with each other despite their claims. So, while the computer majors have tended not to develop applications software (this work has been left to fast moving opportunistic companies – see next chapter), they have developed operating systems which are sold along with their computers.

Since an Operating System is software (and stored on a magnetic tape or disk) it will represent the best programmer efforts as at a certain date. But the manufacturer will continually be improving it as customers get experience with it and start reporting problems and suggestions. To enable their customers to benefit from such enhancements the manufacturer will not sell the operating system as a one-off deal – rather the customer will buy a licence for an annual fee plus the option to buy upgrades and new versions. This arrangement has the added advantage to the manufacturer of being able regularly to milk their customers, and also to keep in touch watching for signs of wanting to expand, change or upgrade the existing computer system.

As the Data Processing department in a company matures – the company computer system, the applications software, the operating system, and the people needed to run it – it will gradually develop into an efficient unit. (Even computer systems can be organic.) This will be achieved as programmers and analysts iron out problems in collaboration with all the people who use and rely on the system. The process results in a sort of fusion between computer and company as the structure and design of the operating system and the applications software pervades more and more company decisions. The onset of this is viewed by the computer manufacturer as a sort of market *rigor mortis* which they want to prevent happening. One strategy they use goes like this: as an Operating System gets old (like the computer it runs on) the manufacturer will give warning that they soon plan to stop maintaining it – i.e., that it is becoming obsolete. Such an announcement sends shivers down company spines that are using (and happy with) the condemned system. In some situations where this has happened a third party company sees the opportunity, offers to buy the rights to the operating system, and to continue giving the same service. The computer manufacturer can simply refuse to sell the rights – and usually does refuse – because the aim behind the announcement is to rock the boat in dusty DP departments, and force the company to get rid of their old computer, and buy a new one – preferably from the same manufacturer!

COMPUTER CONVERSION OF ADMINISTRATION

Back to the story. Let's assume the company's management have negotiated the complexities of the purchase decision. A new computer is installed, complete with Operating System, Payroll software, word-processing, plus database and report-writing software. A few cables are also laid throughout the office building waiting for VDUs to be attached. The additions to company staff include a DP manager, a computer operator (person with skills in making the computer run, etc.), and a computer programmer/analyst. The company have also put the consultancy company on a retainer to handle the conversion task which is planned in phases for the year ahead.

The next task is to specify fully and precisely the projected computerised administration system. This means designing all the files – what information goes in each one – how that information can be retrieved – who has access to what – levels of security – storing of archive information – the creating of regular reports for management – the design of systems to enable new information to be entered and old information to be changed, and so on. The software purchased will be flexible up to a point and accommodate most of the company's needs – but it will never *exactly* fit. The process of reconciling what the company did in the past, with what it wants to do in the future, and the constraints imposed by the software, takes many months of systems analysis work and management decisions. It is a balancing act which demands:

- all management stay informed about the changing implications for their work as computerisation proceeds
- all management contribute to the design so that no gaps appear later
- company "peculiarities" (functions which don't lend themselves to the developing software system) are either dropped or retained in their present manual form
- management recognise the new sorts of jobs that will be created to run and use the new system properly.

Almost without exception the computerisation process throws the company into crisis. People have two jobs at once – one for the computerisation plus their usual old job – and they are expected to get things done in the same time. Inevitably delays creep in and mistakes are made.

To minimise the possibility of completely grinding to a halt, computerisation is usually done in phases. Thus the admin department computerisation might be phased as follows:

- personnel records
- training requirement
- pay, tax and pensions
- word processing

The thinking behind the phasing will be that the money matters are the most important – so they have to be got right. Therefore leave them till experience is gained with something easy like the personnel records. Leave word processing till last – it's seen as popular by the typists and so they'll put inside pressure on the pay and tax staff to get their conversion done smoothly and quickly. Phasing creates divisions, and the more there are the less the risk of collective action to defend jobs.

CONVERSION IN DETAIL

Let's assume we're into phase three – wages and taxes. What actually happens during the conversion? By now the actual work details of all the pay staff will have been raked over and sorted by the computer systems analyst people through a process of interviews, work studies and filing cabinet rifling. Inevitably, however, details describing exceptional events – such as new recruits joining in the middle of a government-inspired tax change crisis – will be missed.

The design will specify how the analysed tasks will be computerised, how the resulting system will be used to do the same work as before, and where additional labour will be needed to cope with the exceptional cases that *have* been identified and which cannot be squeezed into the system at reasonable cost. Any task that cannot be computerised – and it's the systems analyst that helps make this judgement – causes intense management irritation as they see their anticipated savings dwindling in the face of old jobs being retained and new ones created.

The programmers then adjust the payroll software package to accept the agreed design. This can be very quick – in terms of weeks. The next job is to input all the necessary data. Since the personnel data is already stored (because of the phasing in this example), the remaining details required will be minimal – NHS number, tax code, salary, pay review date for example – and the Inland Revenue provide free advice if it's needed. The process of data entry demands existing staff labour – to collect the information and check it after it's entered. But do they get the job of entering it? Are they retrained?

Now that the computer pay system is complete and up to date it is usual to run the old and new in parallel for a while to make sure everything's running smoothly. This is the last opportunity for the old pay staff to shift onto the new system – because in a very short time their jobs will have ceased to exist.

THE NEW JOBS

Once the crisis of conversion is over there is still a lot of work – apart from the actual running of the computer and its overheads – that has to be done by people. Taking the payroll side as an example:

- handling the exceptions work
- entering new information at a VDU
- producing regular computer reports, distributing them, and filing them manually for reference

- producing special reports on call
- adjusting the system to cope with changes in the budget and new laws
- creating and storing regular archive information (tapes and printout)
- extending the service to employees by taking advantage of other computer facilities.

But who gets these jobs? In some cases it's the programmers – they learn the payroll tasks, do the programming, test the system and are then in a very good position to do some of these jobs – unless of course they want to stick with programming work, but these days the demand for programmers is shrinking. For the previous manual system staff to take these jobs they must insist on:

- proper training in the use of the system
- general education on computer systems
- full involvement in the system design
- full consultation in the creation of the new job descriptions,

as a precondition for their co-operation in the computerisation work.

THE DP DEPARTMENT

Following computerisation the Data Processing department is where all data, its processing and the production of reports is centralised. The computer and its memory systems are in an air-conditioned room, while the people who make up the new admin department communicate with the new filing system from flash new offices equipped with computer terminals.

The manager of this empire will have ready access to all the data and to all the software programs used to enter and process the data. This very powerful new role can be threatening to managers in other parts of the organisation – some may attempt to shield information from it so they maintain control of certain data, others will be tempted into thinking how they can use the computer to help with their work. For example, today's training department is more and more interested in computer-assisted learning which requires the development of special teaching support software. Often, however, the DP department will refuse the training section access to the computer on the grounds that "the computer carries confidential information about the company and about employees

– we can't have inexperienced people using it who might corrupt the data". A further unexpressed concern of the DP department is "can't have this lot learning how to program computers – they might show us up".

In the last few years the frustration felt by the departments excluded free access to the organisation's computer has led to departmental purchases of personal computers. Often these machines provide all the computer power needed by a department or executive, and the software range available is enormous. Their low cost means they can be bought almost out of petty cash – except when large numbers of them are ordered and they compete for the DP department budget. Faced with this threat the DP department argues for "computer data to be managed as a common corporate resource" while the individual PC users claim the increased access, flexibility and software available to them,

Report
Global computing services:
EDS is typical of a new breed of specialist computing organisations which take over and run the DP function of client companies. It developed out of the General Motors US computer department, and is now the single biggest client for IBM mainframe computers. EDS "DP support" operations now span the world. There are various steps in the "DP help" offered by EDS to a typical UK organisation experiencing problems in its DP department. This help ranges across:

– "professional" advice in the running of the department
– being engaged to "re-run" the department
– buying an interest in the company's DP operation
– transferring company DP operations to an EDS computer (based in Dallas, for example)
– selling the UK client computer and installing US communications links
– "re-deploying" existing DP department staff.

The development of expertise in data and processing concentrations of this sort makes what EDS offers very attractive to companies wanting to cut computer department overheads. It is also attractive to multinationals wanting to centralise more and more the detailed operational information needed to run their world-wide networks.

(Ex IBM Salesman)

means they work more efficiently. Today the traditional defensive DP department locked up with its massive mainframe computer looks increasingly under threat as company departments use office equipment budgets to buy their own PCs and operate independently again.

Some say this will be a short-lived freedom as "Local Area Networks" (LANs) are developed to link PCs together, and to the central computer. The interesting thing is that as more people in an organisation become familiar with computing through their PC experiences – the less mystified they are by the DP department and the more pressure they will put on it to offer the services and backup that's needed by the whole organisation.

Summary

- *the arguments used to "cost justify" the installation of a computer in an organisation can be made attractive by ignoring realistic running and conversion costs*
- *large computers are still sold to companies sensitive to the idea of innovation and keeping ahead*
- *it is rarely possible to computerise the work of a company department without the full co-operation of the workers*
- *workers potentially affected by computerisation are able to make informed decisions about their working lives only if they are fully aware of the capabilities and function of the envisaged computer system*
- *computerisation is very threatening to a management deciding on "which computer" and to a management committed to "slipping it past the workers"*
- *IBM computer sales strategies are designed to leave customers and competitors alike with the IBM option*
- *computerisation can introduce structural rigidities into an organisation which are less easy to work with than people and filing cabinets*
- *switching operations from a manual system to a new computer system can take many months and is the time of greatest organisational exposure to crisis*
- *computerisation can cut jobs – especially the boring and repetitive ones – it also creates new jobs, but often management only learn about them much later*
- *DP departments can be very conservative and insular in preventing other departments from using the computer*
- *personal computers and powerful software are used by people bypassing traditional DP department power and control over computer facilities*

Programmer at work

PROGRAMS FOR PROFIT

3

Software Publishing is a new industry which strips out expertise from a workplace or organisation, encapsulates it into a computer program, and then markets it as a substitute on floppy diskettes. The steps in this process are explored here from the consultant's recommendation to the stage where marketing can begin, paying particular attention to the roles of computer workers. The work done by computer systems analysts and programmers is popularly viewed as "inhuman, overpaid and a job-for-life". How true is this image? Are programmers ever exploited?

A decade ago most computer programmers worked with very large computers writing very large computer programs – some of which are still being sold and used. But today the appearance of personal computers, the availability of upgraded models of mainframe and mini computers, and the tendency for organisations to use a diversity of off-the-shelf software packages all mean that the work of a programmer is not so easy to define. However, at the heart of their work are computer programs and the data produced by those programs. An understanding of computer work requires an understanding of how computer programs are made. This chapter is about this process and uses a "Corporate Programming" job as its example.

THE ROLE OF THE CONSULTANT

Most programming jobs start with a consultant being called in and expressing a view about a problem. This person might be employed by the organisation with the problem, or come from a "Consultancy Company". You are allowed to call yourself a consultant when you have either done something reasonably successfully before, or you have learned enough by watching someone else do something. You can only perform as a consultant when you are with people who don't know – or think they don't know – what you know. A major role is to make the person with the problem feel more comfortable. This is achieved in several ways:

- you must appear to understand their problem
- you must appear to know about something that will help
- you must behave in a friendly and sympathetic manner.

Appearances are very important. In fact while the above may seem to be a trifle cynical, the fact is that recognising the need for change is uncomfortable and upsetting. The introduction of new technology is such a threat – to managers and employees alike.

There is a sense of wanting to be told what to do by those who know (. . . Here's the money, just do it . . .), which fights against another sense (. . . show me and I'll do it myself . . .). In the commercial world with all its competitive pressures the consultant is looked to as someone who can smooth the way forward. He or she is usually brought in from outside – it is assumed:

- they will behave "more objectively"
- the outside "professional" embodies "expertise and know-ledge"
- they will know how other companies have solved similar problems
- nobody inside the organisation is trusted.

As a rule a useful consultant is one who "has done it before". Another area where "the client" (the organisation or person with the problem) will need comfort – is to be convinced that the consultant does not have any "vested interests" in the outcome of the consultancy work.

So, the client has a problem and the consultant is brought in to understand the problem. The heart of this activity is discussion, though sometimes it is treated defensively by the client... "See those files and papers? Well, read them and you'll understand – then tell me your recommendation." From the viewpoint of the computer consultant let us follow the questioning process used to assess whether a computer solution is applicable or not:

- what work do you do?
- what other people or processes are involved?
- what seems to be the problem?
- what information or data is at the heart of the problem?
- what happens to the information or data now?
- who else is involved?
- give me an idea of sizes, numbers, volumes, rates, timings.

These are loose questions designed to provoke wide-ranging answers which in turn provide the consultant with further avenues for more specific questions. Note that none of these questions starts with "why". "Why" questions are almost always threatening because they are demanding to answer. A consultant will typically start by seeking descriptive answers – hoping to pick up some facts and at the same time identify the sensitivities of the client – before moving on to seek reasons for things.

"SYSTEM/FEASIBILITY/ COST-EFFECTIVENESS"

In these early sessions the client does almost all the talking – a therapy in itself. Once the consultant feels generally informed it is time to seek more specific "evidence" to help sort from the range of possible options and alternatives, the ones that "make sense". So other information is sought:

- an examination of existing systems (usually paper-based)
- observation of "typical" day-to-day activity
- interviews with other people in the organisation.

What the consultant is trying to do is determine the degree to which the problem activity has been systematised by the client organisation. An activity is usually made into a system, if an organisation is interested in employing people to do the job who are not those who developed the activity in the first place, or if the activity concerns records and information of great importance to the smooth running of the organisation. The more the activity appears to be "a system" the more likely the consultant will recommend a computer solution. A system is made up of a number of things:

- activities which are repeated at regular intervals
- paper-based activities which demand "filling in boxes"
- frequent use of filed information
- repetitive arithmetic calculations.

The "perfect" consultant will run through all the dimensions of this "look" at the problem to determine first of all the "feasibility" of computerisation – i.e., would a computer "tool" actually help? The "typical" consultant builds up a picture of the problem based on past exerience of organisations and then usually attempts to shoehorn the client problem into the mould of that past experience. A willingness to accept innovation and difference is not common in an environment dominated by commercial imperatives.

News Story
A management consultant writes:
"'Show me a system that adds to bottom-line profits and I will show you the system I want.' At a superficial level this makes sense. Governments around the world have picked up the theme with their 'automate or die' message. It is also possible to automate and die."

(Computing magazine, 9/1/86)

Assuming a computer solution is deemed feasible the consultant then moves on to explore whether such a solution would be "cost effective" – i.e., would the benefits gained through computerisation justify the cost?

This analysis demands answers to other questions:

- how much does the present system cost to run (labour, overheads, etc.)?
- how much is lost due to failures in the present system?
- how much expansion is planned for the future?

Other questions are then asked which tend to point to the additional "benefits" gained through computerisation:

- how important is information security?
- how else could the information be applied?
- how easy should the system be to operate?
- how should the system check itself?

The final step for the consultant is "the proposal". This stage results in a costed recommendation based on the consultant's stated understanding of the problem. Here is where the consultant is on the thinnest ice. The client wants precise costings while the consultant is happiest with "ballpark" figures – especially since the proposal will be based on an understanding gained over at worst a few hours' chat, or at best a few days. This is where the real "consultant credibility" begins to emerge as the problem is "quantified":

- how "big" is the problem? (what computer is needed?)
- how "complex" is the problem? (how much programming is needed?)
- how "typical" is the problem? (who will do the programming?)
- how "difficult" is the client? (how easily can they be satisfied?)

Why is the word "problem" used when referring to a departmental or individual job of work? For most people the word "problem" tends to mean something bad – as in "problem child". In the computer world "problem" has the same meaning as the problems children are set in their arithmetic homework. So a "problem" is a description of a situation demanding a "solution". Using terms like these enables the computer people to distance themselves from the human side of what is being computerised, and to see it all in terms of abstract algebraic equations demanding solutions. Now, back to our example...

The client wants a "fixed price" deal – with penalties attached if "the supplier" does not do it right. The supplier wants a "time and materials" deal – "We'll charge you depending on how long it takes, but trust us because it won't last longer than . . ." In practice some sort of compromise is reached between the two.

Let's imagine in this case that the client goes ahead and buys the computer recommended. The consultant here works for a "System Software" company and has proposed they should do the programming work on "the project". The work starts with a "System Analyst" being brought onto the project.

THE ROLE OF THE SYSTEM ANALYST

In broad terms the task of the system analyst is to understand totally every conceivable detail of the activity to be computerised in order to create a software design specification. This work is in four parts:

- defining every different information type in the system
- defining every different information processing activity
- writing down a full system structure definition
- designing an appropriate computer program structure.

One of the important side-effects of this work is to identify those aspects of the client activity which are not fully understood by the organisation's management. These are usually activities carried out by individuals on their own initiative – activities which are tolerated in a "human" environment but not in a computer environment which demands predictability and precision to the last dot.

So it is usually the system analyst who has to confront the sharp end of the organisation's employee relations issues. If employees don't wish to or don't feel able to divulge the precise nature of the job they do – then the system analyst can't complete the system definition. There are many reasons for employee reluctance fully to explain the work they do:

- feeling of owning personally acquired experience
- resentment over giving away something for nothing
- irritation at being forced to quantify their personal work life
- fear of a creeping technology they don't know

VDUs in banking

> – fear of job loss through their skills being absorbed by a computer.

If enough employees refuse to co-operate then computerisation becomes impossible because the system is not well enough understood. Furthermore, the existing system has to keep functioning throughout any computerisation work – effectively doubling the work load of employees concerned and also encouraging management to keep the pressure off for fear of upsetting current operations.

In fact it is a "management problem" to ensure the co-operation of employees concerned. There are a number of ways of getting this co-operation:

- guaranteeing job security
- offering good training in the use of the new technology
- providing accurate information on plans for computer and people work
- creating regraded jobs for computer system workers
- integrating employees into the system design process
- getting a pilot system quickly for people to play with.

> *News Story*
> *DHSS computerisation:*
> *"A triangular battle has developed between the Treasury, DHSS management and the unions (SCPS and CPSA). The Treasury wants to reduce staff by 6,000 before 1988. The DHSS management can 'see where savings can be made – but it will take longer'. The unions demand no job losses and also report a sharp increase in the demand for DHSS services. In this climate no new technology agreement has been negotiated."*
>
> *(Computing 22/8/85)*

Now back to the disciplines of the system analyst in the quest for an information and activity definition which will be acceptable to the computer. In practice today's computers can only ever do one thing at a time – rather different from a group of workers busy in an office – so the analyst tries to describe their actions as a sequence of separate and separable activities – each of which demands certain information and each of which creates new information.

ANALYSING A LIBRARY

Taking an example of a lending library, what sorts of information exist?

- for each book: title, condition of copy, number of borrows, if currently borrowed, date taken out, borrower
- for each member: name, address, joining date, last borrowing date, current titles out on loan, due back date
- new books: title, date requested, date ordered, date promised, supplier
- for each supplier: name, address and phone number.

And this ignores other information needs such as the accounts, budgets, employee pay records, book locations on shelves, and so on. What sorts of activities exist which use the above information?

- loaning out books
- taking books back
- answering questions about book availability
- sending out overdue notices

- getting new titles in
- replacing worn out copies.

The analyst has to refine the understanding of the information even further – for example how many lines will be in the longest address? How many letters will be in the longest address line? Answers to these sorts of questions need to be an appropriate compromise between storage demand and space saving so the address uses the least necessary space in the computer. And the same goes for information activities, for example what does loaning out a book entail?

- checking the member does not already have books out or overdue
- entering the borrow information against the borrower's name
- entering the borrow information against the book titles records.

Perhaps the existing system is based on card index systems. One set for members and another for titles. The above activities involve a search through both boxes – taking out cards – checking – writing in details – putting them back in order. How does the system operate with four people on the counter? What happens when cards fill up?

Having analysed the operation and found what the library staff actually do, the analyst will come up with an overall design for the database which might be:

- a computer file for members
- a computer file for book titles
- the use of unique number codes for each member and book,

and a design for the program used when the librarian loans out books:

- type borrower's number into the workstation from their card
- see from the screen if they can borrow
- type in the numbers from the covers of the books selected,

and the same set of operations from the computer's viewpoint:

- find borrower's number in the file and check it
- enter the title numbers into the borrower's database record
- find all requested titles in the title file and enter the borrower's number into each one plus the date, and the due back date.

This is a simple example but shows the use of code numbers to avoid duplication and to enable cross-reference. In the situation where there are tens of thousands of books, thousands of members, and a small number of borrows per week – the analyst would change the design by creating a third file – the borrowed book file. This would only contain:

- the book code
- the borrower code
- the due back date,

and is often known as the "transaction file". A file like this is created because computers take time to search through files looking for things. So searching to see if a book is borrowed is quicker through the "borrowed book" file than through the whole library catalogue file.

THE WORK OF THE PROGRAMMER

Back now to our corporate client. At the end of the work the system analyst produces the system definition and software design. To be useful it will have been carefully raked over by all concerned – including those workers brought onto the project. The detailed process of research, organisation, analysis, writing up, presentation and discussion is one of the most important aspects of the whole computerisation project.

The more people involved and the more groups represented, the more accurate and complete is the final specification. It will have been discussed and modified to represent the best understanding of the activity possible – combined with the system analyst's knowledge of how computers do things. The computer system blueprint now passes into the hands of the programmers.

The programmer's work is structured by the specification drawn up by the system analyst. This specification will describe all the information components, the files and the processes which the software should be able to perform. For one particular process the specification might state "... get the code number from a keyed-in entry, look through the customer database for it, check the status of the customer in the record, if status is bad display message on screen, otherwise display message indicating transaction can proceed ..." It is up to the programmer how to represent this rather abstract process in the computer language the software is to be written in. And just as people tend to write about the same thing differently so, too, do programmers program differently.

It can be a very creative and satisfying task. When a process is programmed for the first time by typing in a sequence of instructions in the appropriate language, they can then be tested by getting the computer to read them – like an omniscient but unjudgemental presence. Working with such sub-programs, getting them to run properly and produce the expected results, is stimulating and demanding and can be done at the programmer's own speed and in their own time.

MANAGING THE PROGRAMMER

The unpredictability of programmer activity has driven many managers to the brink – especially if they fail to appreciate the craft element of many programmers' work.

Some programmers take special care over the layout of their "code", others test their software to destruction, still others fill their software with descriptive comments so maintenance programmers can find their way round the logic. This "management problem" – how to get predictable productivity out of programmers – has taxed the minds of many "work study" theorists who have produced lots of systems to help managers structure and control the software creation process. The principles behind these controls include:

- break the software into small, self-contained elements
- develop "programming standards" to channel programmer creativity
- develop peer testing so programmers read each other's software
- standardise testing of all sub-programs
- adopt a "house style" for programming to inhibit experimental work.

Some of these systems are now marketed and sold as Management Methods with names such as Michael Jackson, Yourdon, Top Down, Structured Design, and so on. In the case of "critical software", the use of "quality assurance" management systems is common (see Chapter One).

In recent years a number of "program generators" have appeared. These are computer programs in their own right and their purpose is to enable "people who don't know computers to program them". One of the first available was marketed with considerable noise under the name "The Last One" – the implication being "You'll never need another program". In most cases these clever tools were developed by programmers themselves when faced with a rather boring and repetitive programming job. They would then write a program which literally did their job for them – though the resulting programs would usually need fine-tuning by the programmer. These clever ideas are now being exploited and sold to companies developing their own software. They hope to use them and cut their programmer work force. In practice the savings gained are minimal – except in cases where very trivial software is being made.

Let's imagine that our example demands the work of a few programmers over an eighteen-month period. Typically this might involve a year making the individual process sub-programs and the file database, six months pulling all the bits together, and a final month testing it and installing it on the client's computer.

News Stories
Programmer employment relations in Japan:
"A report describing what goes on in a typical Japanese software house reveals they are open plan and very noisy with chatter. There is apparently an old Japanese saying 'Western people are dry with each other but the Japanese are wet' – which means that thoughts and emotions flow more easily in Japan. Most programming staff spend a great deal of their time chattering to each other – appearing to joke and gossip."
(Computing, *17/10/85)*

Programmer employment conditions in Britain:
"In a report describing British software house manage-ment methods one employee maintained that the typical attitude is 'treat the staff like mushrooms – keep them in the dark most of the time and throw the occasional bucket of manure over them.'"
(Computing *magazine, 8/8/85)*

Most of this work will happen in the offices of the "Software Company" on their own computer, far away from the client company. The programmers bring detailed computer system expertise and programming experience to the project. In many cases the closest a programmer will get to the client will be reading the system analyst's design document.

SOFTWARE SATISFACTION

Provided the system analyst has done a good job and written coherent specifications the job of the programmers knocking up the sub-programs will be intensive and rewarding for them. They will spend several hours a day at computer terminals typing in the computer language instructions they have written. The sub-programs will be tried and edited. Computer printout will be produced which will be examined closely for mistakes. Errors are what programming is really about. The satisfaction in tracking down an intermittent error cannot be overstated. But it is true to say that concentrated computer activity does tend to alter a person's outlook on life to an "... IF, THEN, ELSE, DO NOT PASS GO ..." approach. Good for driving a car but not so good for the emotional side of life. In fact, if programmers can be more involved in the system specification work it tends to improve their working life as well as the system spec., since they tend to know the computer better than the analyst does and can feed their experiences back into the system design.

TYPES OF PROGRAMMING

The programming work needed in our example covers a range of areas:

- computer operating system programming
- filing system software programming
- application software programming
- user interface programming.

The last of these involves writing software that generates displays on a screen, or takes typed responses from the keyboard, or produces printed reports – all of the activities which provide the link between the computer system and the people who use it. It is usually during the testing of this software with "real people" that inadequacies in the software design show up for the first time – leading to the first set of change requirements.

The application software does all the process work analysed with the client – it adds things up, compares things, checks things, sorts things in order, and generally does all the spadework associated with the client activity. It is in many situations the de-skilling software.

At the heart of our system are the files of information. It is crucial that they be accurate – and that they are secure. The applications software does some fairly obvious things:

- gets records out of a file

- stores records in a file
- empties old records from a file (archiving)
- creates empty records for new information
- keeps track of how much space there is
- does searches for "lost" information.

In fact, it does many of the activities that clerical staff will have done before.

Since every computer has its own different operating system – because every manufacturer makes its own computers slightly differently – someone has to take the trouble to understand it so all the software produced will fit snugly into the computer and operate efficiently. There are far more operating systems than there are computer languages – sometimes it's hard to find operating systems programmers – unless you've got an IBM! So in our example the job was done off client premises on another computer but using the same programming language as will be used on the client computer (possibly BASIC, COBOL or FORTRAN) – but the two operating systems concerned will usually be different.

SOFTWARE OWNERSHIP

At last it's over. The testing is complete, the manager is happy, the client is happy, training has started, and people are beginning to use the system with all its little sub-programs all furiously working away getting information, processing it, and storing it. Each little sub-program being the fruit of a programmer's inventiveness.

But the story does not end here. Apart from the problems of implementation, conversion and all the little hassles associated with using new technology effectively – who owns the software that has been made?

- the client company which paid for it?
- the software company which made it?
- the workers whose skills are now embodied in it?
- the analyst and programmers whose ideas made it happen?

It is sobering to note that the software packages available off-the-shelf today – for accounting, word processing, filing, etc. – were yesterday's clever solutions to specific client problems. Copies of such software packages are sold in their thousands. Each package is a combination of special filing ideas, inventive screen presentation, and the representation of specific working skills. There are cases where quite large companies computerising their payroll, pension payments or accounts systems, have recognised the wider value of such software and set up separate companies to market it for the use of their competitors. The smart software company can earn rather more from a client than simply the money they are paid to write software. Through careful attention to copyright arrangements they can also gain ownership of the packaged expertise of the client's work practice itself! It makes commercial sense – but who are the winners and who are the losers?

News Story
A solicitor writes about the Computer Software Copyright Amendment Bill:
"'There are those who think that the new Bill will solve all software copyright problems; they are almost certainly doomed to be disappointed... Contract law may be the best way to protect software... Under Copyright law the most important issues are the rights to adapt, publish and reproduce.' He goes on to explain that software fits into Copyright law either as a 'literary work' (on paper printout) or as a 'sound recording' (stored on magnetic tape)! It seems that the best protection is to keep printouts and to devise proof of 'originality'."

(Computing *magazine, 6/6/85)*

THE PROBLEMS WITH THE TYPICAL CORPORATE APPROACH

In this example – which is typical of many corporate programming projects – the people who actually write the software are very far removed from the client workers employed in the "problem" area. This separation inevitably leads to problems:

- there is a risk of programmer effort being wasted through poor understanding of the problem because of poor links with the client workers themselves

- there is a wasted opportunity in involving and educating the workers through not letting them participate more in the programming process
- there will be a reduction in the quality of programmer output due to a feeling of making cogs for a machine
- it is the workers who have the most detailed feel for a work process and if that gut feel is kept away from the software design there is a risk of creating a company millstone
- too much reliance is placed in the system analyst specification being right
- the client investment in teaching outsiders about "the problem" is wasted because they will move on to other jobs and other clients and be lost.

Some would argue that the laws of copyright are inhibiting and restrictive. These people are not photographers, film-makers, song writers or composers. The software industry is highly unregulated and capable of exploiting situations to its own advantage. It is an industry where many people with good ideas or valuable experience are ripped off easily by smart executives. The problem comes in two forms:

- how can programmers benefit from original software designs?
- how can workers prevent their skill from being asset-stripped?

The former point raises the issue of protecting an idea – how can this be done? While the second has a recent interpretation in Wapping – expertise and skills developed over centuries, and handed down from worker to worker (albeit in a rather restricted way!), are now encapsulated in computer software. The question is – who really owns the software? Can the "means of production" be stored on a £5 floppy disk?

THE SOFTWARE SALES INDUSTRY

In fact very few companies have made pots of money from software developed internally to meet their own needs. But the applications areas where significant profits have been made include:

- employee pay systems
- employee pension systems
- company accounting systems
- stock control systems
- general filing systems

running on the larger computers made by IBM, DEC, ICL, Burroughs, Honeywell, etc. Most of the profits have been made by the specialist software companies brought in to do systems analysis and programming work for particular clients. Through their first couple of contracts in an application area – for example, on company pension schemes – the software house learns how companies actually handle employee pensions. They are paid as they learn. Using the profits from the work and copies of the software they have developed – which no law properly prevents them from copying – they can then generalise from the particular needs of that client to produce a generic package which can be sold to other companies with similar needs. Product development is paid for by early clients, and real profits are made in selling copies to other companies eager to gain the same computerisation advantage – without the pain of developing it themselves!

The existence of such software packages encourages companies to buy computers so that they can share in the long-term administrative savings the software embodies. One major problem involved in taking on a ready-made package is that the company will inevitably find their previous practice is not totally represented by the software – so they either have to spend lots of money to modify the software (if the software licensee will allow this), or they have to adjust company practice (see Chapter Two). (Further exploration of the British software industry is presented in Chapter Four.)

Large computer manufacturers like IBM have seen the opportunity that selling generic software represents. Their ready-made market of IBM computer owners has been too good to miss and IBM is at pains to keep competing software makers away from them. IBM have developed software that is used to set up very large data systems such as bank account systems, government data systems and library storage. Once a client is hooked into such an IBM system it is very difficult to break loose from the IBM grip – because doing so would involve converting an enormous software and data investment from one computer to another (a very costly operation). And because the same IBM software is increasingly being used for such data systems around the world, a global network of compatible data systems is developing which allows for

easy data transfer and the potential for communications, takeovers
and transfers which has never existed before.

Summary

- *the lack of commitment to "computer education for all" in many corporate programming jobs leads to the alienation of those who know the task from those who are programming*
- *writing a computer program which fully supplements a work operation or practice demands the fullest possible collaboration and involvement of programmers and workers*
- *the ideal situation where computer power is used by the workers to do their jobs more effectively and efficiently will be undermined by attempts to "program everything"*
- *management will often exploit the divisions between programming staff and other workers to push through changes, thus intensifying the knowledge gap between programmers and workers*
- *management concerns at uncontrollable programmer productivity have led to the use of "design methodologies" and "program generators" to divide and separate programmer activities – often to the detriment of the software being produced*
- *programmers working in isolation from the intended users of the software work less effectively, and risk temporary concentration problems due to lack of human contact and excess computer work*
- *software workers' programs embody their creative efforts in the same way films are "owned by the makers" – but software copyright allows easy duplication without bending the law*
- *computer software can be made to represent the skills of workers – thus benefiting the group that "owns" the software, but not the workers whose skill is replaced or the programmers who programmed it*
- *the widespread use of a very small number of software packages is leading to increased standardisation of social and work practices and information organisation. Much of this software is designed in the USA and so its use has a growing "Americanising" effect*

"Computers at Work"

CURRENT COMPUTING CONCERNS

4

A one billion pound deficit in the balance of payments annually. A statement that VDUs present no health and safety problem. A law regulating the privacy and use of personal data which gives the police full exemption and the employer more rights than employees. What do these events have in common? They are all results of Thatcher government "intervention" in Britain's software and computer applications industry.

This section explores some additional topical issues and concerns affecting the British software industry and its computer workers in the late 1980s. The treatment is cursory and serves to highlight the main arguments as well as indicating other references on the subjects covered – which include:

- the state of Britain's software industry
- the health and safety problems confronting VDU workers
- the Data Protection Act.

THE STATE OF BRITAIN'S SOFTWARE INDUSTRY

Government trade figures published in 1985–86 show a trade deficit in the software industry approaching one billion pounds. Yet the popular conception is that British programming expertise is the best in the world – why is Britain doing so badly? To look behind the software scenes it is useful to divide the industry into two parts:

- "the bespoke software industry" – where programmers are employed to write software specific to a particular customer's needs
- "the software package industry" – where pre-programmed software for generic applications is sold off-the-shelf.

It is argued by certain British software companies that Britain is doing very well in the former industry – particularly on the international market – leading to a positive effect on the balance-of-payment figures. The reason this is almost certainly true is that German, French, Dutch, American and Japanese programmers are all paid far more than their British equivalents – so Britain will use its own labour force for British work while other countries in the West are more than happy to exploit cheap British labour. In fact while some of this labour may lead to the production of "quality" software products, the bulk of it is "engine room programming" where old software is upgraded or converted to a new operating system or new computer, for example. It is very rare for imported British programming labour to be used in the development of "secret" new software designs and software products. In the USA, APPLE and IBM rely on Americans for this work – people they can trust not to take original ideas out of the country. The Japanese in their government-funded fourth generation software initiative rely on their own talent – while carefully considering any other ideas generously provided by other Western countries invited to the table (whose main intention is to sniff out Japan's ideas!).

So Britain's "bespoke" labour force abroad is attractive to foreign employers:

- for doing mundane programming jobs cheaply and efficiently (they speak English, after all – which is the language of the
  computer industry)
- because they might provide an idea that can be exploited
  once their contracts are over and they go home.

This is not to deny the importance of programmer employment in the software industry (and a large number of "bespoke" programmers never leave Britain's shores for work) economy equation. But it does highlight the fact that there are all sorts of programming industry activities – ranging from the simple profits made from low cost software programming through to the long-term benefits of software product investment.

Software imports vs local indusry

It is in the latter category that Britain is rapidly falling behind in a quickly expanding world market. Why is Britain slipping despite its reputation for good software engineering and design ideas? Perhaps this reputation is not deserved. After all, most of the remarkable software developments – such as the first APPLE operating system, the APPLE MAC series of software products, and SPACE INVADERS, owed nothing to British thinking. And a casual look at the lists of software packages available for computers of all sizes – from massive mainframes to desktop PCs – reveals that almost all of them were made in the US and are marketed either from there or from British offices and shops under US licence. Why this imbalance?

News Story
Personal computer software publishing in the US:
"With more than 27,000 different computer programs now available for the IBM personal computer, any new software company faces enormous difficulties getting to the market. Distribution is increasingly difficult as High Street computer retail shops open up and shut down unpredictably... After-sales support is crucial. Mail order is proving successful too – along with a concept called Shareware – where copyright is lifted and copying is encouraged in order to establish a user base."

(Computing, *10/7/86)*

It is unlikely that the imbalance can be accounted for by saying that Americans have more or better ideas than the British. The difference lies in how the ideas are handled and exploited. What is needed to move into the off-the-shelf software market is:

- investment in fully finished software product development
- investment in software product marketing
- investment in software product distribution,

and it's only when these investments have been successful nationally that a British company can use that experience and expand its market internationally. A lot of British software is "rough and ready" and "brutal" – essentially unfinished. It's mainly through the process of marketing that potential users' needs and concerns surface and serve to stimulate the changes and enhancements needed to ensure the product is attractive and useful. This is where the Americans come out on top with their enormous concern for "the customer" and customer service, and the software products being made by small companies there reflect this concern. Britain's local software makers need stimulation, imagination and support to fully develop and market their software throughout the country.

News Story
A systems programmer writes:
"Most systems development focuses on problem solving to the exclusion of everything else. This usually produces code which performs the specified function but is totally unusable in practice... More emphasis on presentation – the human interface, will improve productivity and in some cases bring the application within reach of the users."

(Datalink, *29/7/86)*

Future opportunities

The next ten years will see continuing massive investments as Britain's public service sector becomes more computerised. This is an enormous slice of the national software market which is gradually being colonised by foreign multinational software products – due to a lack of commitment to Britain's indigenous industry. And this developing software market is of crucial importance to society in Britain – let alone the software industry! Take local government, for example. Each of the hundreds of local authorities throughout Britain have to administer annual budgets in the vicinity of £100,000,000 and manage the tenancies of up to 100,000 council homes. Efficiency and speed of service in these areas would be hugely enhanced with the use of properly designed computer systems. The social service and community labour that could be potentially made available through computer assisting certain admin activities would also be considerable. In time this will all happen. Unfortunately, however, the motivation behind recent Conservative government enthusiasm for computers in the Civil Service has been cuts. This also means a cut-price approach to computerisation itself. When looking into computerising the Inland Revenue studies were conducted showing it was worth spending £200,000,000 if it meant cutting 10,000 jobs – as one firm of software consultants said, "You don't get a good system design if you start from the position of paying for the system by job cuts."

What is needed is a strategic approach which looks into the wider benefits of computerisation for society as a whole and for the people public service organisations have been set up to help. All too often the drive behind the software design is to make cuts rather than to provide services more efficiently and fairly. Good public service computer software packages could be marketed to countries which share similar forms of state organisation – just as India (rightly or wrongly) bought into Britain's paper-based service control systems many decades ago.

HEALTH AND SAFETY PROBLEMS OF VDU WORK

VDUs have now replaced pen and pencil for over two million workers. Many have experienced health problems due to the ways they have to work with these new tools.

Computers haven't been around for long, and so the long-term effects of working with VDUs are poorly understood, especially the effects of any electrically stimulated emissions from VDUs. This "evidence problem" is like the one concerning the risks of low level radiation to the public – is it "safe" to dump waste into the sea or not? Perhaps a hundred years from now our scientists will be much clearer about what the actual risks are/were – but today the most

Keyboard work likely to lead to Repetitive Strain Injury

pragmatic worker's response to a possible risk is to treat it as a real one.

In summary the major health and safety risks perceived and reported from working with VDUs are as follows:

- problems with pregnancies – such as miscarriages and babies born with abnormalities
- sore eyes, eye strain and peculiarities in focusing
- aches and pains in the back, neck, arms and legs
- repetitive strain injuries to finger, wrist and arm tendons
- skin rashes
- anxiety, exhaustion and stress
- decline in motivation and interest in the work.

Of these problems the risk to pregnancy is the most controversial and has attracted some scientific attention. Following union pressure a study (known as the DHSS Runcorn study) was conducted which suggested the risk to women of miscarriage, stillbirth or malformation was DOUBLE for VDU workers. For various reasons – such as small numbers in the study sample – the civil service and other experts regard the survey's findings as inconclusive. However, the Council for Civil Service Unions issued a statement in August, 1984:

> "We must stress that the current state of medical knowledge is uncertain. Nevertheless the Runcorn study, however suspect, means we cannot discount the possible risk to the foetus from VDU work. We therefore recommend that those members who are concerned that there may be a risk from VDUs should, on request, be transferred to other work."

News Story
Report on Government VDU Safety Booklet:
"The Government's Health and Safety Executive says in its booklet Working with VDUs *that the screens are not a hazard if used properly. There is no evidence, it says, to link VDUs with either eyestrain or miscarriages. This view flies in the face of the VDU Workers' Rights Campaign which is lobbying for legal regulation of VDU use. The author of the booklet said he saw no need for legislation. 'The health complaints that come in are determined by so many different things that you could never have legislation to cover it,' he said."*
(Datalink, *17/2/86)*

SOGAT '82 and NALGO are among the unions which have successfully negotiated agreements with employers which require that concerned VDU workers be transferred temporarily to other jobs during pregnancy. In other countries, most notably USA and Sweden, these sorts of agreements are fairly commonplace now.

The health problems listed above are not experienced by every person operating a VDU, and in many cases it has not been possible to attribute the cause of a given problem to any one single aspect of VDU station operation. However, it is possible to identify a number of VDU station design and operation characteristics which contribute to health problems. It must be emphasised that the importance of these factors varies from application to application and from VDU to VDU, but there are risks attached to all of them.

Pregnancy problems

- electrostatic and electromagnetic field emissions from VDU equipment (NB – these are not the same as atom bomb radiation, but studies indicate they do have an adverse biological effect).

Work environment problems

- reflections of windows and lights in the VDU screen causing glare and obscuring parts of the information display
- small or fuzzy text used making it difficult to read the screen
- desk surface too low or shaped so there is nowhere to put papers
- seating does not allow foot resting or stretching of legs
- chair doesn't allow easy adjustment for height or backrest
- keyboard layout poor, or too thick, causing awkward wrist movements
- printer noisy
- room conditions too hot, cold or dry
- electric shock problems due to static.

Work operation problems

- insufficient break times from intensive VDU work
- long-term risk to wrists and fingers due to very repetitive keying-in work.

Work quality programmes

- no social contact involved on the job
- omniscient computer boss always hungry for the "in tray" to be emptied generates a feeling of relentless pressure
- poor software design so VDU workers feel they are just correcting or compensating for a poor system, feeling they could do it better but never being allowed to
- no opportunity for ever making a decision.

The work environment problems are being looked at very closely now in Britain, and there's no end of manufacturers trying to flog their own "solution to the problem" – helping managers to appease their staff with cheap gimmicks. Good equipment and designs are not cheap and don't come easily, and no amount of "ergonomic expertise" should be allowed to substitute for the views and experiences of the workers themselves. Solutions to operational problems come in the shape of agreements over how much time in total should be spent in a working day in front of a VDU, how long should each burst of activity be, how long for breaks, and how to share the different keying-in jobs around so workers don't get locked into a rigid set of key movements for life (which are reproduced in dreams and remembered in wrecked tendons). Typical union/employer agreements for this vary depending on the intensity of VDU work (keying-in data off paper is intensive, handling phone enquiries using a VDU is less intensive), and average around four hours VDU work per day, and also ten to twenty minute breaks for each VDU hour worked.

The work quality problems are more subjective and more ignored. One VDU data entry clerk deliberately introduced errors into her work so she could go and talk to somebody. This is a creative response to the social alienation that computerisation and VDU work can bring. For a job to be satisfying – rather than soul-destroying – it requires personal contact, variety and some independent discretion. These requirements bring together job design and software design – each must take account of the other for the best combination.

THE DATA PROTECTION ACT

In the 1960s and 1970s public concern about the volume and use of information collected about individuals led to several Private Members' Bills being submitted in parliament – all of which were aborted. Eventually a Labour government set up a committee to investigate this issue, which published a report in 1975 entitled **Computers and Privacy**. It outlined the committee's views on what they felt computers could be made to do:

- facilitate the administration of extensive record systems
- enable the data to be quickly and easily accessed from a distance
- enable the speedy transfer of data from one system to another
- make it possible for data to be compared and examined in ways previously regarded as impracticable
- allow for the coding and encryption of data so few data workers would know the nature of their job.

This work led to the Lindop Report on Data Protection in 1978 and – after increased EEC pressure – to the Data Protection Act which became law in 1984. Britain now has a Data Protection Registrar and the law requires that ALL users of personal data in computer form register with the office. There are few exemptions and the regulations are detailed and wide-ranging.

Early reactions

Recently the union APEX (Association of Professional, Executive, Clerical and Computer Staff) made a statement about the Act which read:

> "APEX welcomes the Data Protection Act and the appointment of the Data Protection Registrar. We see the Act, however, as only one step towards the safeguarding of personal privacy. We have expressed our disappointment that the Act does not go as far as the comprehensive legislation which has been passed in Europe and North America, and we feel there will be a need in the future for further legislation to enable us to come into line with world opinion."

In broad terms the purpose of the Act is to regulate the use of files of personal information held on computers. Early committee investigations suggested there were nearly half a million such systems in Britain ranging from small CAB office computers with information on a few hundred regular visitors, to vast systems such as the police "criminal" record files. The Act requires personal data on computers to be registered, to be accurate, relevant, not to be disclosed to others, and able to be checked by the data subject. (The term "Data User" describes the organisation "owning" the computer data, while the term "Data Subject" applies to an individual recorded in a computer system.)

The computer press are carrying a growing volume of reports expressing dissatisfaction with many aspects of the Act:

- small data users are finding the Act to be complex, difficult to interpret, and very time-consuming even to fill in the registration form
- more data users are concerned that compliance with the maintenance and administration requirements of the Act is excessive and very costly
- almost every organisation which has registered has come up against ambiguities in the Act which they are free to exploit in their own interests
- trade unions and individuals are concerned about the scope of the privacy protection provided to individuals.

In summary it seems that large corporations are worried because the Act will increase their computer overhead costs (job creation), while progressive organisations and individuals are worried because the protection offered is vague and incomplete.

Aspects of the Act

Before looking at some of these concerns in more detail it is instructive to examine the provisions of the Act.

Certain types of data are exempt from the Act:

- domestic data (home computing)
- text processed data (word processing)
- non-personal data (not relating to individuals)
- corporate data (company information)
- manual data (any information not in a computer)
- national security data (to safeguard "national interest")
- payroll, pension, accounting data.

The latter category is exempt provided it is not disclosed, and provided it is not used for any other purposes. If, for example, a company used its pay data files to store additional information about employees (e.g., personal tax code, NI number, lateness, sickness holiday records, promotion, disciplinary action) then it would have to be registered and employees would have the right to check it.

There are different **types** of personal data that can be held about a data subject and which are recognised by the Act:

- factual information –
    names, addresses, religion, membership of an organisa-
    tion, etc.
- opinion information –
    appearance, attitudes, creditworthiness, employability,
    prospects, etc.
- intention information –
    information about what the data user intends to "do" to/
    about the data subject.

Intention information is exempt from the Act. So, if "J. Smith is to be arrested" or "J. Smith is to be made redundant in three weeks", is the computer data filed under J. Smith, then J. Smith could never discover this under the provisions of the Act.

Individual rights under the Act

Other major provisions of the Act concern the rights of data subjects in respect of data stored about them:

- access, the right to see data held about them (after November
    1987!)
- accuracy, the right to seek compensation due to the use of

inaccurate data, and to have it erased
- non-disclosure, the right to seek compensation where data is lost or where it is disclosed illegally.

All of these points may be enforced through the equivalent of the English High Court, but generally they will be "policed" by the Data Protection Registrar following "non-trivial" complaints from data subjects. In fact many personal data files are exempt from the "access" clause by the Act, for example:

- files used to prevent or detect crime
- files used to apprehend or prosecute offenders
- files used in assessing or collecting tax
- files used in judicial appointments
- files used for "legal purposes"
- files containing certain health and social work information.

News Story
The Data Protection Act and the medical profession:
"Individuals will have the right to check their own medical records after November, 1987. This clause of the Act has proved unpopular with doctors, and the British Medical Association has voted against patients having this right. Doctors were worried 'patients would misinterpret what had been written about them'. A psychiatrist has said, 'If all records become published (under the Act) I think every doctor will keep a second set of manual records'."

(Datalink, *29/7/86)*

Some specific concerns

It is increasingly felt that the Data Protection Act treats personal data as the private property of the data user, and gives data subjects very little say in how information about them is used. This list contains various specific concerns that have already been reported:

- personal data is defined as excluding all data not processed automatically. Some users are therefore transferring all "sensitive" data to manual/paper systems which are only INDEXED from the computer – thus exempting all such data from the Act
- the distinction between "opinions" and "intentions" in the Act allows sensitive data to be expressed as "intention", and therefore to be exempted from the Act

- data subjects have the right to check which organisations
  their data has been (or might be) disclosed to. However, the
  combination of the data user listing all disclosure POS-
  SIBILITIES (in case one is ever needed) plus the fact that
  certain disclosures are secret and therefore not accessible to
  the subject, can mean the disclosure register is meaningless
- the act of registration itself is filled with ambiguities (due to
  the slap-dash way the Act was put through Parliament),
  which means that the information held by the registrar is
  likely to be inaccurate.

Summary

- *Britain's software industry is in steep decline leading to
  severe balance-of-payments problems; reduced job opportunities for skilled computer workers; the creation of a market
  for the foreign software industry; the invasion of American
  culture represented in the structure of US-designed computer
  programs*
- *much original software development is "done in the garage",
  and demands strategic investment to bring it to the market, to
  promote it and to distribute it – this is not happening*
- *aspects of Britain's service and local government sector would
  be made more effective and efficient through using computer
  tools. The necessary software should be developed in
  association with the community to provide socially responsive
  software which would in turn be marketable internationally*
- *VDUs do constitute a health hazard for many reasons causing
  a range of problems – the risk to pregnancy cannot be
  discounted*
- *VDU workers suffer due to physical aspects of VDU work; due
  to operational problems such as insufficient breaks; and due
  to the decline in work quality that accompanies a dehumanised approach to computerising*
- *the mental health problems associated with poor software
  and job design are largely ignored at present – they lead to
  stress and depression at the very least*
- *the Data Processing Act does improve individual rights in
  respect of computer information being stored about a person –
  but there are still many loopholes enabling the Act to be
  exploited in favour of organisations rather than individuals*
- *the Data Protection Act needs to be updated to take account of
  specific problems experienced with it, and to bring it up to the
  same level as equivalent laws in other parts of the world.*

Learning by doing

COMPUTERS FOR THE PEOPLE

5

The previous sections contain descriptions and observations about the application of computers and computer software in organisations whose major concerns are cost-cutting, profit and the shareholder. The primacy of these concerns over others – for example employee working conditions and the quality of a service – inevitably dictate the way computers are used in such environments. However, computers don't have to be used to the detriment of people's working lives. It is possible to learn from commercial experiences and from various "alternative" experiments, to draw out ways of working positively with computers.

Starting from the premise "computers can be good for you", this chapter examines computer applications, activities and approaches which go some way to putting people first. Three perspectives are presented:

- illustrative applications
- computer assisting the small organisation
- a social agenda for the software industry

ILLUSTRATIVE APPLICATIONS

Local government computerisation

This is beginning to happen now in a fairly **ad hoc** way, and unless a strategic approach is taken there will be a lot of wheels being re-invented. One of the most crucial problems for local authorities is the administration and organisation of council housing. Some authorities have already attempted to computerise these activities. One such authority has been quick to recognise that nearby authorities would also benefit from their software. However, lack of dialogue meant the different criteria they each used for allocation were not recognised. Consequently the resulting software was rather awkward to use by any authority other than the originating one.

This problem could repeat itself round Britain – leading to unnecessary expenditure. Housing allocation software – if it is to be developed strategically – needs to take account of these potential policy differences while at the same time bringing out the common features. Using this software a given local authority would ideally be able to customise its housing system to take account of its specific needs, while taking advantage of the embodied common features.

The development of such software cannot be left in the one-eyed control of a software company, nor can it be directed alone by an ivory-towered local authority bureaucracy. The software design should start with the needs of people – thus the change to new technology can be used as a lever to make a quantum leap in improving the services to a community. Then the software people and the local authority officials can take up the "social specification" and create a system which meets real needs.

Enhanced diabetic care

The London New Technology Network (LNTN) is one of the software "garage industries" started by the GLC before it was abolished. Among the many products that are being developed is a software package from the Enhanced Diabetic Care project. This started because of the problem that many diabetics have in getting advice from their local GP, since most relevant knowledge is centralised in hospitals. A collaboration of the DHSS and GLEB provided the finance while the Medicine Department at St Thomas's hospital in London provided a large database of diabetic case histories as background material. Workers at the LNTN are developing the software package in consultation with the medical profession and GPs – and the aim is to produce a tool that will help GPs offer a better consultation and advisory service. The software works as an "Expert System and represents current "best practice" in the field.

The major difficulty with this sort of project is in encouraging GPs to take it up. To do so they have to buy a computer plus the package.

They find it difficult to justify if all the system will do is help with diabetics. This is the classic Hifi/LP problem – is it worthwhile buying a record player if there's only one record? One answer is – it depends on how much you like/need the record. In practice there are many aspects of a GP's job that could be greatly improved through the consultative development of further packages such as patient lists, medication lists, as well as other "best practice" software assistants. The existence of a library of GP software would benefit GP and patient alike.

It is useful to summarise some of the GLC's aims in supporting and stimulating software industry development:

- in conjunction with London Boroughs the GLC will investigate the specific needs of local authorities and public services for computerisation over the next ten years
- the GLC will investigate further the options for opening up an international distribution channel for software
- the GLC will develop packages for the voluntary sector which better fit their needs than commercially available systems
- through various training schemes the GLC will seek to extend knowledge of computers and the use of software to women, black people and people with disabilities
- the GLC will campaign for a shift in state spending on software development from military systems towards the funding of civil applications.

Trade union membership lists

Some trade unions have already computerised their membership lists on large computers housed in national headquarters buildings. Others are cautious. The big brother image of centralised computer lists, some well-publicised abuses of personal information access (not in trade unions!), and the current law-driven trend away from delegate decision-making to private ballots – have all combined in creating an atmosphere where the use of computers in a trade union is regarded with deep suspicion.

This atmosphere can be dispelled provided all concerned have the fullest possible knowledge of computers in general; the fullest contribution in specifying exactly how the computer is to be used; and full knowledge and control over how it is used once installed and set up. Emphasis is placed on knowledge here because without it the opportunities offered by a carefully-thought-out member information system will be missed, or delayed for a long time.

The cautious approach is to store the very least information possible about each member:

- name
- work address
- joining date
- last subscription payment date (possibly).

There are other opportunities, however. How do trade unions go about checking how successful their policies and campaigns have been in actually changing things? For example, if a union was active in encouraging employers to discriminate positively in favour of women, black people or the disabled – as new recruits, for promotion, or in the provision of new skill training – how would they check the effectiveness of such campaigns?

This sort of analysis is assisted if the appropriate information is available. To meet this possible "measurement" requirement and to deal with other typical possibilities, a more comprehensive membership list would be needed:

- name
- age
- home address
- ethnic origin
- sex
- disability
- dependants
- annual wage
- weekly hours worked
- annual pension contributions
- employment type
- employment address
- job type/level
- health and safety concerns
- training needs
- trade union branch code
- local trade union representative.

Every year each member would be contacted by their trade union representative at work (or at home) to fill in a form so the computer list is kept up to date. The actual categories and headings within the system would be defined by the trade union to fit in with their objectives, and the database would be designed to take additional categories as new needs and issues arose. In fact the above list is fairly simple as databases go (use the Data Protection Act to examine the data held on you by your bank, for example!) – since it is often useful to have several different databases which interlink, giving greater flexibility and cutting down on repeated information (for example, the local trade union representative might be named in thirty members' records).

To avoid understandable criticisms of centralisation and destruction of the branch a further possibility is to link trade union branches or regions into the central computer by means of desktop PCs over telephone lines. These PCs could be used locally for word processing (newsletters, notices and meeting agendas); for communicating information between the HQ and region; and for access to the branch's membership list – e.g., to enable the branch representative to keep that part of the central member database up to date.

For such a system to even happen it is crucial that all concerned be made aware of the possibilities first, so that collective decisions can be taken in an informed atmosphere.

COMPUTERS AND THE SMALL ORGANISATION

Getting started

While there are no accepted rules or moral guidelines for "computerisation without tears", there are several collective processes which should be planned as part and parcel of the computerisation timetable. These steps have been drawn from the experiences of people in organisations where such steps did not happen, and from people who made them happen. Among them are:

- computers, software and programming are part of a new technology understood by a small percentage of the population. Therefore it is crucial to improve people's involvement by initiating a full education programme to improve "computer literacy" in the workplace. This should include seminars, good print material, videos (good ones available on hire) and as much "hands-on" experience as possible
- computerisation should not be seen as "applicable to admin. only". Rather it should be regarded as a tool for use across the organisation. This means throwing open the

entire organisation for analysis and examination. No stone should be left unturned – the "favourites" must be encouraged to co-operate so everybody gets the same treatment

- any analysis and specification document should be available to everyone so they can criticise its accuracy and contribute to it. This specification should describe all the current work practices fully so everybody can learn what everybody else does, and see how they fit in. This is a pre-requisite to deciding what and how to computerise
- the computer system document should be used as a sounding board and receptacle for the collective view of the organisation – a view that is informed by understanding of computer applications. The process of producing it will be consultative as all reactions and ideas are taken acount of, and the system definition is refined
- whether writing new computer programs or using existing software packages, ensure the route taken is as flexible as possible to enable changes later on. This means using fairly open-ended software which is never really "finished". Commitment to this approach demands the organisation has continuous access to programmer staff to meet new needs arising, and enables the computer system to develop dynamically as the organisation changes – rather than being a confining millstone
- once the computer system is contributing to the organisation (returning the investment banked with it by the other workers) then its design and method of use should be fully written up in the sort of guide a new person joining the organisation could pick up and use
- as the computer becomes more and more integrated into the organisation – as people use it more and more – then that use can be widened and expanded as people feel they are free to explore different ways of using collected information to gain different perspectives on the organisation's work.

These broad aims have at their heart the desire to stimulate involvement, to maximise diversity, and to ensure it is people that control the computer and not the other way round.

Moving towards computerisation

Not every organisation automatically benefits from the use of a computer tool. A self-employed acupuncturist seeing one patient a day probably needs a computer about as much as a hole in the head. Yet there is a pervading feeling – especially with the availability of low-cost personal computers – that an organisation is incomplete without one. In fact many organisations run well, if not better, without the overhead and hassle of a computer system. So, the first recommendation is: "don't buy a computer until you know you need it". If you think a computer might be useful then the first thing to do is spend some time talking to people in similar organisations who are using computers already:

- what work does the organisation do?
- what aspects are computer-assisted now?
- what computer systems and software are they using?
- are there any problems with their system?
- what expert help did they get in choosing it?
- what help did they get in setting it up?
- how long did it take before it was working for them?
- what new software had to be developed?
- what training did staff need?
- were new people recruited?
- how much expert help is needed with day-to-day running?
- what maintenance and insurance is needed?
- will the system meet their plans for development?

They may also be able to advise you on where to get more specialist help, or give you contacts for any expert work you need to buy in temporarily. Talking with people who don't want to sell you anything is the best way to learn. It is also very important to find out from them how much **everything** costs:

- how much was the hardware?
- how much was the software?
- how much did it cost to design the system?
- how much did creating the system design on the computer cost?
- how much did converting the old system onto the computer cost?
- how much did any new programming cost?
- how much does it cost to run now?
- how much is maintenance and insurance?

and the biggest question of all:

- if you did it again, how would you do it differently?

Assuming computerisation is a possibility the next thing is to write down what people in the organisation feel they want to be able to do with a computer:

- what existing jobs could be computer-assisted?

Word Processing in the office

- what existing book systems or file systems could be stored in the computer?
- how is the new computer system to be designed?
- who is going to do the conversion work?
- who is going to operate the system when it's finished?

There is an understandable desire to handle all aspects of the computerising using the knowledge already in the organisation, and based on the popular idea that "anyone can work with a computer". In fact installing a computer system – for the accounts, for filing systems – is a task which demands expertise so that it can be done quickly and well. Unless there's someone about with that knowledge and experience then someone has to be found who can provide the help required to take the next steps:

- draw up a budget for software and hardware selection
- work out a plan for creating the full software system needed
- advise on the conversion process of the existing systems.

These decisions then lead to:

- what software packages will be needed?
- what information will need to be stored, and how?
- how will the system be used, and by whom?

Applications and software choice

Small companies are capable of carrying out a bewildering variety of activities and so there are no easy answers to the question "What software?". On the other hand, there are some fairly standard activities which do lend themselves to computerising and lots of software alternatives have been developed for them:

- word processing
- accounts
- filing
- stock control
- business planning.

The problem for a company is not so much which ones to buy, but how are any different software packages going to work with each other, in parallel with the way existing company employees and systems work together. Off-the-shelf software products tend to be very self-contained and difficult to "open up" in any way that would enable them to "communicate with" other software packages. So the choice of software tends to be:

- choose highly-specialised software, divide the company traditionally and apply the software to each division
- choose a software package which "does everything" in its own way, and change the company to suit
- write your own software
- a mixture of the above.

In the past these problems were intensified because there was only one very large computer which had to do everything – leading to all sorts of compromises and to very central organisation. The advent of personal computers has undermined that by decentralising computer power to the individual users who are free to apply their computer as they want – without being shoe-horned into the common interest computer This causes its own problems if an organisation's efficiency or strength is embodied in the information it has – since it will tend to be disorganised and fractured across various personal computers. Local networks of personal computers can be applied in alleviating this. By contrast certain applications are very highly specialised now and demand decentralisation. Word processing is such an application where custom-made hardware and software comes together as a package. Some of these are so cheap it often makes sense to have separate word processing systems, and other computers for accounts, for example – particularly when there are several workers using them.

The accounts

The great thing about an accounting software package is that it encapsulates many of the straightforward skills that traditionally have been sought from the company's accountant. A properly set up accounting system can quickly and easily provide the company with extremely useful information about how they are doing, while also cutting down on the time needed by outside accountants in "doing the books at the end of the year". A further benefit is the education gained by employees in understanding the accounting disciplines and in rigorously organising their own accounts.

The typical small company operates with the simplest of accounting systems:

- a sales book ledger
- a purchase book ledger
- a filing cabinet full of invoices,

It has the odd panic in working out the quarterly VAT return, and hands the whole lot over to the accountant at the end of the year. The Thatcher years have taught most organisations to be aware of

Computerised Accounting in the small organisation

costs and to control expenditure carefully – be it a public or private concern. But unless a lot of time and energy is put into the company's accounts – breaking them down by department, by project, by product, by service, by month, etc. – then there is little possibility of real control over company finances.

A major benefit of most computerised account systems is the use of "nominal ledgers". These are convenient account control slots that can be defined by the company to suit their own organisation. Nominal ledgers can be created for each; cost centre, profit centre, project, production, product, service, department, etc. And when purchases or sales happen they are automatically passed to the appropriate nominal ledger. This means it is possible to check how EACH aspect of the company is doing at any time, plus all the other benefits offered, such as automatic VAT return calculations, profit and loss sheets, weekly returns and all the rest!

Some of the more expensive accounting systems are available in modules and you choose what you want, such as:

- sales ledger
- purchase ledger
- invoicing ledger
- nominal ledger
- stock control
- payroll
- project costing.

Some packages even stray into "non-accounting" areas such as stock control, automatic ordering and employee pay slip printing.

Special applications and documentation

For "common" applications a huge range of software is available. Buying a popular seller is usually a good idea because it will mean the package is "well supported" and well tested, with telephone-help available and included in the purchase price. There are hundreds of less well known packages available for all sorts of applications – many of them reviewed and for sale through W. H. Smith-type computer weeklies and some for sale in the High Street computer shops. Reliance on peer group experience is the best way to wade through these possibilities – some of which can lead to disaster.

User documentation is almost always a disappointment – unless the software comes from APPLE – and takes a long time to understand. Once a system has been implemented on the company computer it makes a lot of sense to write a company system user guide for everyone else to use.

A SOCIAL AGENDA FOR THE SOFTWARE INDUSTRY

In this last part of the book the various threads of argument introduced earlier are brought together for consideration by several different groupings:

- industry
- trade unions
- education

Industry

"The person in the street currently sees the UK software industry now and in the future as a high growth, export revenue generating industry, contributing significantly to UK employment and the balance of payments. This view is wrong." This statement is drawn from a 1986 report written by a team of software professionals which included directors from several top British software companies. They further argue that the very low levels of support and planning in Britain's local software industry has left the door wide open for US multinationals to jump in and successfully market American products. Among the crosses the industry has to bear are:

- despite the Thatcher government's stated commitment to IT, very little money has been invested in the software industry, and no strategic guidance has been available
- there has been government investment in the military software industry but most of what is produced is either not socially useful or is kept secret in "the national interest"
- cutbacks in nationalised industry spending and in private industry have all hit corporate software research projects
- educational cutbacks have hit universities like Salford which are at the heart of Britain's "new software ideas" industry, and which are forging links with industry
- Britain's large software companies like Scicon and Logica are not able to attract the investment required to take some of their products fully finished and developed into the market-place – hence they lose out to more polished American products
- too often software development is linked very heavily with

particular hardware systems (the IBM approach) in the hope that such system owners will buy the software. The reality is that good software which meets real needs will always be attractive and can always be converted

- now that much of Britain's software market (PCs through to mainframes) has been fed on a diet of American software, they will have become used to the taste and won't be keen to change
- a lot of Britain's software is just not designed with a human being as a user in mind – it may have a good "engine" but it almost always has very poorly designed "controls". Many of Britain's software producers don't realise what their users are looking for...

There are no easy answers to these problems. But here are some progressive attitudes to adopt when making software:

- the best software comes when real efforts are made at bringing "user" and "programmer" together at every stage in software production

VDUs in a local authority

- a distinction needs to be made between Britain's local software industry and the "export" market. How is it possible to make an export product without having first tested it on – and satisfied – the local market?
- the production of good software is an expensive and labour intensive process. It needs upfront investment. Britain's own "garage industry" of software makers need support before their ideas are snapped up by grateful multinationals
- the computerisation of Britain's public and local government services is one of the most crucial areas of software opportunity. Provided early development projects can be guided by the desire to provide services fairly, fully and efficiently – rather than merely to cut costs – then the resulting software will be of real benefit and use throughout Britain, and probably other countries.

News Story
Parliamentary report:
"A Tory backbencher has denounced as 'crazy' figures showing that despite the UK's economic decline fifty-one per cent of spending on research and development by the government is acounted for by the Ministry of Defence (MoD). Crawley MP Nicholas Soames insisted that 'the absolute maximum proportion of the amount of government R and D in defence should be twenty-five per cent, and the balance should be distributed between the DTI and DES (Industry and Education) so that we are like most other mature countries'."

(Computing, *29/7/86*)

Trade unions

Britain's trade unions have traditionally sought to protect workers' jobs and to regulate and improve working conditions. The widespread application of computers and computer software – often to cut jobs – has naturally led unions to adopt a defensive attitude against their over-enthusiastic use by greedy employers. Today a large and growing proportion of the workforce work very closely with computer systems. In addition the quality of many of Britain's public services are heavily dependent on enormous computer systems. The combination of these two influences is leading many unions – particularly certain union research departments – to critically and creatively examine the role of computer software in defining workers' jobs and in meeting public needs.

A major difficulty has been the organisation and unionisation of the programmer and analyst workforce. This has not been a success – partly because many of these workers feel well paid and secure, and partly because the new and complex issues confronting this sector of the workforce have not been fully recognised.

News Story
Report on unions and computer workers:
"Because of their failure so far to convince DP staff of the advantages of joining a union, unions are shifting the emphasis of their campaigns towards issues which are of more immediate concern to staff in the computer industry. A spokesperson for ASTMS said, 'we have had to adjust our approach, and focus on one-to-one contact between union representatives and individual members. Our approach has to be based on the first principle that we know about the industry.'"

(Computing, *1/5/86)*

Every worker is affected by computers today – even if it's only an Inland Revenue computer. Different concerns affect different groups of workers – programmers, VDU operators, and all employees recorded in computerised personnel systems. Among these concerns are:

- the Data Protection Act needs to be exploited fully by employees concerned about the use and accuracy of personal information held by their employers. However, employees can only exercise this legal right if they are informed about the Act.
- VDU operators do face physical health risks from their equipment. In addition the nature of their work can be reduced to such a dehumanised level because of software designs that they risk distressing mental health problems as well
- when jobs are threatened by computerisation then the bargaining power of job knowledge needs to be used as a lever in gaining maximum computer education and training for all concerned – this has the knock-on effect of structurally ensuring that EVERY aspect of the job is taken into account so the resulting software BEST supports the work
- full involvement between programming people and workers is crucial in identifying every function which will NOT be

computerised OR which will need labour. Computerisation is as much about defining the new jobs needed as it is about defining the computer system

- the job satisfaction of programming workers is considerably increased if they have the chance to meet with/work alongside the future users of their software. Their software will be better for it also. These links need to be fought for across union divides
- the use of "design methodologies" and "program generators" needs to be actively questioned – especially where it over-shackles the programmers and adversely affects the resulting software
- the copyright law for computer software is inadequate and leaves the door open for software workers' ideas to be freely and easily exploited by "owners".

Education

Attitudes and ideas about computers and software are formed in many ways. The education system has an enormous role to play in promoting a wide-ranging understanding of the role of computers in society:

- any organisation which claims to offer education about computer software technology should balance the typical scientific and technical approach with a treatment of the social and personal side of the industry and its impact
- the general education available at school for everybody should include a treatment of computers and computing which highlights the fact that it is people who control computers (and not vice versa), and which would be based on an examination of the steps in a series of computerisation case-studies
- education needs to be provided for the huge majority of the population who are past "school leaving age", and who are increasingly having to work with/live with a technology which is alien and often frightening to them
- an educational approach which treats computing only in terms of bits, bytes and Fortran leaves trainees without much of the background required to make software which meets the needs of people and which is designed to be used by people.

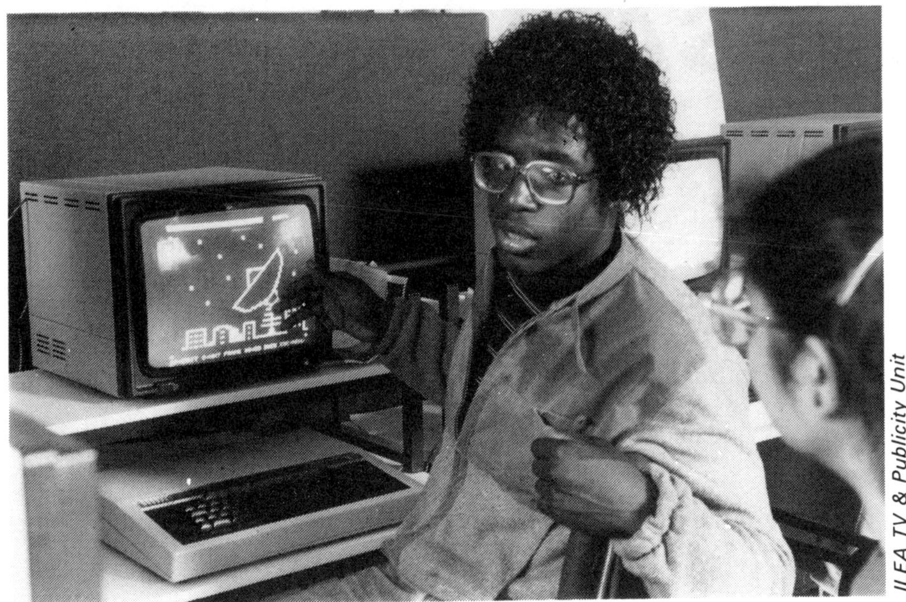

Computers in schools

95

GLOSSARY

This is a very brief glossary serving to describe the technical terms that arise in this book only.

Chip – an integrated circuit. There are two main types: microprocessors which are tiny computers, and memory chips which store data.

Data – another word for the information which a computer can be programmed to collect, store and process.

Disk – the magnetic circular devices used to remember data and programs. These come in the form of "floppy disks" when they are in paper envelope covers and "hard disks" when built into the computer itself.

Diskette – as for disk, but usually applied to "floppy disks" and other disk formats that can be slotted in and out of the computer.

Mainframe – the name given to the very large computers made by IBM and its competitors. They usually run many terminals, sometimes over phone lines or satellite links.

Minicomputers – the name given to computers that are between personal desktop computers and mainframes. Minis usually stand on the floor and run a few terminals.

Printer – the device used for printing out information stored in the computer.

Program – a set of instructions for a computer to carry out. Usually written in a computer language such as COBOL, FORTRAN or BASIC.

Software – similar to Program – the instructions that make a computer work. Software usually comes in "packages" on floppy disks with user guide manuals.

Terminal – a combination of keyboard and screen used by a worker to put information into a computer, to get it out, and to make or run computer programs.

VDU – short for Visual Display Unit. The screen where computer data is displayed, and where information entered using the keyboard is displayed. There is usually one of these with each terminal.

USEFUL PUBLICATIONS AND VIDEOS

The Chip At Work (1981): Published by TUC, Congress House, Great Russell Street, London WC1B 3LS.

Computer Software: The London Industrial Strategy (1985): Published by GLC, available from the London Strategic Policy Unit, Middlesex House, 20 Vauxhall Bridge Road, London SW1V 2SB.

VDUs, Health & Jobs (1985): Published by Labour Research Department, LRD Publications, 78 Blackfriars Road, London SE1 8HF.

Data Protection Act (1984): All information from: Office of Data Protection Registrar, Springfield House, Water Lane, Wilmslow, Cheshire SK9 5AX.

Data Protection [Guidelines] (1985): APEX, 22 Worple Road, London SW19 4DF.

Four UK computer industry papers published weekly
Computing
Datalink
Computer Talk
Computer Weekly

USEFUL VIDEOS

New Technology – Whose Progress (1981 – Riverfront Pictures) "Robots, computers, CAD-CAM, databases, are all going to change our lives. *Whose Progress* examines who will benefit from all this technology. The video draws evidence from critics and proponents alike. It is lavishly illustrated with shots of systems at work, and shows the way television has equated new technology with progress."

Technology At Work (1982 – Education Media)

"A shop floor view of new technology from Metal Box, Cadbury, Tesco, the DHSS and Sheffield Housing Department. The video tells a frank and not always optimistic story, but it is one which provides lessons for others to learn."

Working Terms (1985 – Team Video)

"In this closely observed study, the women working in Tameside Met. Council, their union reps, and their managers all reveal their different attitudes as new technology is introduced for clerical and typing work."

Repetitive Strain Injuries (1984 – Video Projects)

"This video explores the range of work practices which can result in the painful disease – Tenosynovitis. Through interview with mainly women workers suffering from this affliction, the video investigates how incorrect equipment design, work rates and bonus systems can all be contributing factors."

Bliggens Last Stand (1985 – Video Projects)

"This dramatic reconstruction explores the computerisation of a whole company's admin department and serves to depict the attitudes and actions of worker, manager, and union rep. All of the issues that typically crop up are revealed in a light-hearted way as the drama unfolds for the last employee to embrace the computer."

All distributed by: TEAM VIDEO, 2 Ridgemount, Ridge Road, London NW2 2QX.

APPENDIX 1

THE SOFTWARE WORKINGS OF A COMPUTER

To get the best out of a computer it makes sense to understand what the elements of a computer system are and how they work together. A typical computer system consists of two main things in jargon known as:

- hardware (actual boxes and lumps of equipment)
- software (computer programs of various sorts stored on disks)

The hardware is made up from several different items:

- a screen for displaying information and for checking what you type
- a keyboard for typing in words or numbers
- a disk system for reading programs or information off disks – or for storing information on disks
- a processor unit (the bit that "thinks") for using application programs to process information
- a printer for producing reports or letters and so on.

Computer software comes in three main types (don't be surprised if this is not immediately clear – it will become clear soon . . .), which come stored on diskettes or tape casettes:

- application programs which are designed to handle accounts, word processing and information filing, for example
- data, for example pages from a report, account information, and address lists
- the operating system.

Generally, application programs are written in one of a very limited number of computer languages (BASIC, PASCAL, COBOL – short for Commercial and Business Orientated Language!) – and in principle may be used on lots of different types of computer. The reason this never is as simple as we are led to believe is because every type of computer is different in some way from every other computer – surprise, surprise in the free market! The guts of any computer is lots of transistors and semiconductors connected together needing to be told what to do, and these instructions come from the operating system software in the first place. And the operating system is told what to do by the application program, which is directed by you sitting at the keyboard. In fact, the workings of a computer are very much ankle-bone connected to the knee-bone stuff.

You may wish to skip these next two sections, but they are intended to give a better understanding of the way a computer does what it does – two aspects are considered:
- how the computer memory works
- what happens when you write a letter on the computer.

There are three main types of computer memory:

- the memory in the processor unit which only works when the computer is switched on, and which is used to hold the bits of information you are working on as well as the application program you are doing the work with
- the memory on "diskettes" which hold either application programs or files of data and information. Their memory is permanent unless you decide to erase or copy over old information – just like an audiocassette
- the memory on the "hard disk" which is housed inside the processor unit normally. This works in the same way as diskettes – except the hard disk holds much more information and allows you to get at it much more quickly.

On to the next part – what happens when you go to your computer to word process a letter?

- you switch the computer on
- without you noticing, it reads the operating system software off disk and into its processor memory
- the operating system fiddles around getting the date and the time, then it reads the word processing software off a disk (you have told it to do this) and into the processor memory alongside itself
- the operating system then tells the word processor to get started, so it does and displays its first message to you on the

screen

- you say you want to write a letter, the word processor gets your keyed-in message and works out it will need empty space on a disk to put the letter, so it asks the operating system if that's OK
- the operating system checks the disk, first to see if there's an available one in place, and second to see if there's enough space
- if everything is OK it tells the word processor to continue
- you see the message from the word processor and you start typing
- the word processor takes your words from the keyboard and into the computer processor memory space left. It then formats the words appropriately and asks the operating system to display them on the screen so you can see what you are typing
- gradually the leftover computer processor memory fills up as you type more words. Both the operating system and the word processor keep a check on how much is stored, and when there is a good-sized batch the operating system is asked to take them all and put them into a storage space on the disk – and all the time you type oblivious to this fury of organisation and order.

So, the operating system is very important in the workings of a computer. But as far as you, the user, are concerned, the only software you should need to learn about are the applications programs you buy to do the jobs you want computerised. EXCEPT under certain conditions...

WHEN TO WORRY ABOUT THE OPERATING SYSTEM

There are certain things you may want to do which are very dependent on matters concerning operating systems:

- carrying information to another computer on diskette
- connecting computers together in a network
- transferring software to a bigger or smaller computer
- using different sized diskettes (storage capacity)

– using special software which only "talks" to a limited number of operating systems (i.e., not yours).

These are all questions of "compatibility" – you cannot plug a lightbulb into a wall socket, yet they both work on 240 volts. The reason for all this is that each computer manufacturer uses different hardware technology to make their computers, and will also have developed their own operating system software so that programmers can actually use the computers. To avoid problems of copyright and to try to protect their segment of the market, each manufacturer is interested in the maximum compatibility difference that will keep existing customers, alongside the minimum overall differences, to encourage users of other computers to change over. Quite a balancing act – and one which gives computer users endless headaches.

APPENDIX 2

HOW INFORMATION IS STORED AND REPRESENTED IN COMPUTERS

Information storage is at the heart of how a computer works. An understanding of this shows just how stupid computers are, and how much work human beings have to put in to get computers to do anything at all useful. All information and processes stored in a computer have to be converted to the form that computers work with. Computers run on electricity, so all information has to be converted into a form that lends itself to electrical signals. Simply plugging a microphone into a computer and talking to it is not readily possible yet (but the engineers are working on that one very hard – imagine what that will do for word processor operators!)

Today's computers work by converting everything into binary code. This is a code made up only of 1s and 0s. Our alphabet has twenty-six letters and our number system has ten digits – we use these thirty-six characters (or codes) to codify much of what interests us. Even with this variety there are many aspects of life which are not described well – our emotions, for example. But the computer has only two characters to work with and so anything we want computers to do has to be converted into 0s and 1s. Within a computer, 0s and 1s are represented by a flow of electricity for a "1" and no flow for a "0" – rather like switching a light on and off in a special sequence to communicate a message. Needless to say, different computer makers adopt variations in how As, Bs and Cs should be represented in 0s and 1s inside their computers – hence problems in compatibility – one standard conversion is called ASCII.

The problem for code makers started with our alphabet and number system, and then moved on to punctuation (commas, quotes, etc.) and other things like brackets and asterisks. They settled on a sequence of eight 0s or 1s as the base of the code system – so, for example, a "Z" might be 01101011, and a ")" might be 01010111. And this was agreed and became a standard, variations of which are used by all computer manufacturers.

An interesting tangent is the work pursued in creating a world standard vocabulary and grammar. The work put in to standardise codes for the alphabet and so on has also been carried out for grammatic structures – the aim being to establish clear mathematical rules for sentence structures in various different languages. In English, for example, this work is at the heart of trying to get computers to "speak", to "listen" and to "write". A bigger problem is translation. IBM produces reams of documentation describing its computer systems in English – but not all countries are happy to work in Engish, despite IBM's wishes. So IBM is trying to get over this problem by deriving rules for the inter-translation of technical text from any European language to any other. The aim being to computerise the production of technical documentation into their market's languages. What they have found is that the sheer magnitude of the problem has forced the vocabulary size to be kept below 3,000, otherwise today's computers cannot cope – and most of those words are computer jargon. (A typical adult has a vocabulary of around 10,000 words.) The energy and money behind this work will continue to exert substantial pressure for standardisation and for the minimisation of difference.

So far, we know that words, numbers and symbols have to be converted into strings of 0s and 1s to be processed in a computer as a sequence of electrical pulses. But how are they stored on a floppy disk? The technique of disk storage is the same, no matter if it's a hard disk, a floppy disk or a cartridge. It's all done with magnets. When a computer disk is running it spins around at great speed. An arm moves across the spinning surface to read information or write information to a particular track on the disk – this is very similar to a record player, where the stylus can be placed to play the track you want to hear – it's different in that you can't record a song on an LP!

Let's say you have typed a client letter into the computer and you want to store it on disk. First of all the operating system checks the first track on the diskette to find out where there's an empty track on the disk (there may be other letters stored there). Provided there is an empty one the arm moves to it and then starts recording the letter onto it. The letter will come out of the computer as a sequence of 0s and 1s (electrical pulses), and it is recorded onto the disk as a row of little magnets – some pointed one way (for 1s) and the rest pointing another way (for 0s). This is possible because the disk's surface consists of a magnetic coating effectively made up of millions of little magnets which can be turned to point where required. Thus the letter is stored as a sequence of magnets along the chosen track (or many tracks if it's a big letter). The operating system then records the name of the letter in the directory at the beginning of the disk and the job is done. Reading the letter again is simply the reverse process – the reading arm detects the magnets and converts this information into the same string of 0s and 1s as were stored. And, of course, any letter (or whatever is stored on disk) can be recorded over (just as audiocasettes can be erased and used again).

Because disk storage is based on magnets, then heat or the proximity of other magnets can destroy what is stored by causing all the little magnets to line up in another direction.

APPENDIX 3

VARIATIONS IN PERSONAL COMPUTER SIZE AND PERFORMANCE

If you've got more than £20,000 to spend on a computer system then this section probably won't be much use to you. But if you're thinking about a personal computer system of some kind then there may be some useful hints here. The main technical variables that concern the users of a computer system are:

- processor speed (time taken to perform calculations and manipulate information)
- processor size (measure of the complexity of application programs that will run in the processor)
- access time (measure of how quickly information can be located and retrieved from disk storage)
- storage size (measure of how much information can be stored on diskettes or on hard disks).

Processor speed and size is largely determined by the semi-conductor technology incorporated into the "thinking" chip. So an "eight bit technology" based computer is slower and less powerful than the next size up – a "sixteen bit technology" computer. Sixteen bit computers come with varying sized processors – a small one would be sixty-four kilobytes and a big one would be 512 kilobytes. They all work at more or less the same speed, but the bigger they are the more complex the application program they can run.

Access time for retrieving stored information is determined by the disk technology used – a floppy disk is slower than a cartridge diskette, which is slower than a hard disk system. Some operations – such as address lists and typical databases – require rapid access to stored data, otherwise the delays can be irritating.

Storage size is measured in kilobytes also, but what is a kilobyte? One "byte" of storage is big enough to store a single letter or digit of information. A kilobyte of storage is big enough to store 1,000 letters and digits – or approximately 200 words (in an address system each address – name, initials, addressline, 1, 2, 3, 4, etc., postcode, phone number – might take about 200 characters). So a typical 500 kilobyte diskette can hold 100,000 words or about 200 close typed pages of information (or 2,500 addresses as described above). Hard disk storage capacities are specified in megabytes – millions of bytes – an average hard disk system can store ten megabytes of information, which is equivalent to 4,000 pages of information – it sounds a lot but some applications really eat up storage – after all, it's only twenty or so novels, and think how many books there are in a library!

Organizations and Democracy Series